Terrorism

CRIME, JUSTICE, AND PUNISHMENT

Terrorism

Ann G. Gaines

Austin Sarat, GENERAL EDITOR

CHELSEA HOUSE PUBLISHERS
Philadelphia

Frontis: Rescue workers amid the rubble of the
Alfred P. Murrah Federal Building in Oklahoma City.

Chelsea House Publishers
Editor in Chief Stephen Reginald
Managing Editor James D. Gallagher
Production Manager Pamela Loos
Art Director Sara Davis
Picture Editor Judy L. Hasday
Senior Production Editor Lisa Chippendale

Staff for TERRORISM
Senior Editor John Ziff
Associate Art Director/Designer Takeshi Takahashi
Picture Researcher Patricia Burns
Cover Illustration Takeshi Takahashi

First Printing

1 3 5 7 9 8 6 4 2

The Chelsea House World Wide Web site address is
http://www.chelseahouse.com

Library of Congress Cataloging-in-Publication Data

Gaines, Ann.
Terrorism / Ann Gaines; Austin Sarat, general editor.
    p.   cm. — (Crime, justice, and punishment)
Includes bibliographical references and index.
Summary: Examines the history, mentality, goals, and acts
of terrorists and discusses what a free society can do to pro-
tect itself against them.

ISBN 0-7910-4596-X (hardcover)

1. Terrorism—Juvenile literature. 2. Terrorism—Prevention—Juvenile literature. [1. Terrorism.] I. Sarat, Austin.
II. Title. III. Series.
HV6431.G24 1998
364.1—dc21   98-20190
                                                 CIP
                                                 AC

364.1

Contents

CRIME, JUSTICE, AND PUNISHMENT

Fears and Fascinations:

An Introduction to Crime, Justice, and Punishment

By Austin Sarat

We live with crime and images of crime all around us. Crime evokes in most of us a deep aversion, a feeling of profound vulnerability, but it also evokes an equally deep fascination. Today, in major American cities the fear of crime is a major fact of life, some would say a disproportionate response to the realities of crime. Yet the fear of crime is real, palpable in the quickened steps and furtive glances of people walking down darkened streets. At the same time, we eagerly follow crime stories on television and in movies. We watch with a "who done it" curiosity, eager to see the illicit deed done, the investigation undertaken, the miscreant brought to justice and given his just deserts. On the streets the presence of crime is a reminder of our own vulnerability and the precariousness of our taken-for-granted rights and freedoms. On television and in the movies the crime story gives us a chance to probe our own darker motives, to ask "Is there a criminal within?" as well as to feel the collective satisfaction of seeing justice done.

Fear and fascination, these two poles of our engagement with crime, are, of course, only part of the story. Crime is, after all, a major social and legal problem, not just an issue of our individual psychology. Politicians today use our fear of, and fascination with, crime for political advantage. How we respond to crime, as well as to the political uses of the crime issue, tells us a lot about who we are as a people as well as what we value and what we tolerate. Is our response compassionate or severe? Do we seek to understand or to punish, to enact an angry vengeance or to rehabilitate and welcome the criminal back into our midst? The CRIME, JUSTICE, AND PUNISHMENT series is designed to explore these themes, to ask why we are fearful and fascinated, to probe the meanings and motivations of crimes and criminals and of our responses to them, and, finally, to ask what we can learn about ourselves and the society in which we live by examining our responses to crime.

Crime is always a challenge to the prevailing normative order and a test of the values and commitments of law-abiding people. It is sometimes a Raskolnikov-like act of defiance, an assertion of the unwillingness of some to live according to the rules of conduct laid out by organized society. In this sense, crime marks the limits of the law and reminds us of law's all-too-regular failures. Yet sometimes there is more desperation than defiance in criminal acts; sometimes they signal a deep pathology or need in the criminal. To confront crime is thus also to come face-to-face with the reality of social difference, of class privilege and extreme deprivation, of race and racism, of children neglected, abandoned, or abused whose response is to enact on others what they have experienced themselves. And occasionally crime, or what is labeled a criminal act, represents a call for justice, an appeal to a higher moral order against the inadequacies of existing law.

Figuring out the meaning of crime and the motivations of criminals and whether crime arises from defiance, desperation, or the appeal for justice is never an easy task. The motivations and meanings of crime are as varied as are the persons who engage in criminal conduct. They are as mysterious as any of the mysteries of the human soul. Yet the desire to know the secrets of crime and the criminal is a strong one, for in that knowledge may lie one step on the road to protection, if not an assurance of one's own personal safety. Nonetheless, as strong as that desire may be, there is no available technology that can allow us to know the whys of crime with much confidence, let alone a scientific certainty. We can, however, capture something about crime by studying the defiance, desperation, and quest for justice that may be associated with it. Books in the CRIME, JUSTICE, AND PUNISHMENT series will take up that challenge. They tell stories of crime and criminals, some famous, most not, some glamorous and exciting, most mundane and commonplace.

This series will, in addition, take a sober look at American criminal justice, at the procedures through which we investigate crimes and identify criminals, at the institutions in which innocence or guilt is determined. In these procedures and institutions we confront the thrill of the chase as well as the challenge of protecting the rights of those who defy our laws. It is through the efficiency and dedication of law enforcement that we might capture the criminal; it is in the rare instances of their corruption or brutality that we feel perhaps our deepest betrayal. Police, prosecutors, defense lawyers, judges, and jurors administer criminal justice and in their daily actions give substance to the guarantees of the Bill of Rights. What is an adversarial system of justice? How does it work? Why do we have it? Books in the CRIME, JUSTICE, AND PUNISHMENT series will examine the thrill of the chase as we seek to capture the criminal. They will also reveal the drama and majesty of the criminal trial as well as the day-to-day reality of a criminal justice system in which trials are the exception and negotiated pleas of guilty are the rule.

When the trial is over or the plea has been entered, when we have separated the innocent from the guilty, the moment of punishment has arrived. The injunction to punish the guilty, to respond to pain inflicted by inflicting pain, is as old as civilization itself. "An eye for an eye and a tooth for a tooth" is a biblical reminder that punishment must measure pain for pain. But our response to the criminal must be better than and different from the crime itself. The biblical admonition, along with the constitutional prohibition of "cruel and unusual punishment," signals that we seek to punish justly and to be just not only in the determination of who can and should be punished, but in how we punish as well. But neither reminder tells us what to do with the wrongdoer. Do we rape the rapist, or burn the home of the arsonist? Surely justice and decency say no. But, if not, then how can and should we punish? In a world in which punishment is neither identical to the crime nor an automatic response to it, choices must be made and we must make them. Books in the CRIME, JUSTICE, AND PUNISHMENT series will examine those choices and the practices, and politics, of punishment. How do we punish and why do we punish as we do? What can we learn about the rationality and appropriateness of today's responses to crime by examining our past and its responses? What works? Is there, and can there be, a just measure of pain?

CRIME, JUSTICE, AND PUNISHMENT brings together books on some of the great themes of human social life. The books in this series capture our fear and fascination with crime and examine our responses to it. They remind us of the deadly seriousness of these subjects. They bring together themes in law, literature, and popular culture to challenge us to think again, to think anew, about subjects that go to the heart of who we are and how we can and will live together.

    *   *   *   *   *

Nothing strikes fear into the heart of an average person more than the image of a plane bombed out of the sky, a building destroyed, a bus attacked. Terrorism is the distinctive, though by no means unique, crime of our age. It tests the limits of rational crime policy by challenging reason itself. Terrorism defies limits, conventions, norms. It deals in death, death that can strike anyone, anywhere. In simply leading our lives, going about our business, none of us is safe. Or so the terrorist would like us to believe, because the strategy of terror is a strategy of fear.

Terrorism begins with the story of Pan Am 103, an airplane destroyed by terrorists. It details the careful, time-consuming efforts of investigators to piece together the puzzle of that shocking tragedy. The story of Pan Am 103 provides a vehicle through which we can understand the history of terrorism. This history, which takes us all the way back to the days of the Roman Empire, is a complicated record of people responding to oppression or advancing zealously embraced causes.

But *Terrorism* is more than a book about the past. It provides a rigorous examination of the varieties of modern terrorism and of the groups that have used it. In addition, it gives us a close-up look at an individual terrorist, an opportunity to see the world through his eyes. It reminds us that terrorism is a problem for Americans as well as for citizens of other nations. Because the fragile fabric of modern society is particularly vulnerable to terrorism, the challenge for all of us today is to find new ways of combating this form of crime while preserving the hard-won protections and freedoms that terrorism threatens.

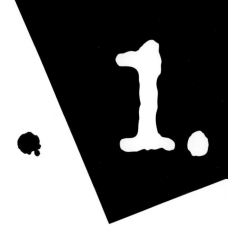

EXPLOSION OVER LOCKERBIE

A t 6:25 P.M. on December 21, 1988, a Boeing 747 jumbo jet taxied down the runway of London's Heathrow Airport and took off. On board for the London–to–New York leg of Pan American Flight 103 were 259 passengers and crew, most of them American citizens returning home for the holidays. In seven hours they expected to land at John F. Kennedy Airport in New York City.

The flight plan called for the jet to fly north over Scotland while gaining altitude and speed, then to head west over the Atlantic Ocean. At 7:19 P.M., just as the plane reached its planned altitude of 31,000 feet and its cruising speed of 550 miles per hour, air traffic controllers at Heathrow saw the small green blip that represented Flight 103 disappear from their radar screens.

Scottish police carry the body of one of the 259 passengers who died when a terrorist bomb brought down Pan Am Flight 103 near the small town of Lockerbie.

A scene from the Reign of Terror, during which the revolutionary government of France executed an estimated 40,000 citizens. Although the word terrorism entered the English language in reference to this period, by definition government repression, regardless of how severe it may be, does not constitute terrorism.

In Lockerbie, a small Scottish town just over the English border, several horrified eyewitnesses watched as a burning jumbo jet dropped from the sky and crashed into a field just outside town. Pieces of the plane rained down over a wide area, and several large chunks fell on houses at the edge of the field. Eleven Lockerbie residents were killed by falling debris, and hundreds more were treated for injury and shock. All 259 people aboard the jet died.

Aviation accidents, though comparatively rare, take a toll on our sense of security. At the back of every air traveler's mind lurk images of a sudden and fiery death, and an activity that otherwise would be completely routine becomes a source of anxiety. But the crash of Pan Am Flight 103 was no accident. It was a carefully planned and meticulously executed act of terrorism.

Though the phenomenon of terrorism is much older, the term first appeared in the English language in 1795, when the statesman Edmund Burke delivered a famous speech before the British Parliament in which he denounced "those hell hounds called terrorist." Burke was referring to the revolutionary government of France, which between March 1793 and July 1794 executed an estimated 40,000 of its citizens—many of them for ideological "crimes against the people"— during a period that would come to be known as the Reign of Terror.

Today, over 200 years later, governments themselves aren't called terrorist, but a precise definition of the word is still elusive. In 1986 the antiterrorism task force headed by then–Vice President George Bush put forth a definition that captures many of the essential ingredients. Terrorism, it said, is

> [t]he unlawful use or threat of violence against persons or property to further political or social objectives. It is usually intended to intimidate or coerce a government, individuals, or groups, or to modify their behavior or politics.

The U.S. State Department's official definition adds that terrorism is "perpetrated against noncombatant targets by subnational groups or clandestine agents, usually intended to influence an audience."

Terrorists commit a variety of crimes to achieve their goals. These include assassination and murder, bombings, hijacking, kidnapping, the destruction of property, even bank robbery.

It's important to emphasize what terrorism is not, however. It is not government repression, even when that repression takes the shape of random and bloody actions intended to strike fear in the hearts of the civilian population. As the State Department's definition makes clear, terrorism is committed by *sub*national groups. Distinction also must be made between terrorists and guerrilla movements. Guerrillas seek to overthrow a government by organizing a fighting force that will grow into an army, gain control of progressively larger areas of the countryside, and ultimately win a military victory over government forces. Terrorists, by contrast, hope isolated acts of terror will achieve their political goals, and despite grandiose names that often incorporate terms signifying a large fighting force, such as *brigade* or *army*, they typically work in small cells of 10 members or less. Muddying the distinction somewhat is the fact that guerrilla movements sometimes use terrorism as a tactic; nevertheless, the thrust of their activities is the achievement of a military victory.

Terrorism is a weapon of the weak against the strong. While no Palestinian group can directly challenge the might of the Israeli military, for example, a campaign of suicide bombings can undermine all Israelis' sense of security. The victims of terrorism are often random civilians. In part this is because civilians are easy targets, in part because the randomness of the victim can have a huge psychological impact on other members of the targeted society: it shows everyone that they are vulnerable, just as the airline passenger might wonder, however briefly, whether his or her particular flight could go down. This is not to say that terrorists never strike military targets. In 1983, for example, a suicide bomber drove a truck full of explosives into the barracks of U.S. Marine peacekeepers in Beirut, Lebanon, killing 241 American servicemen. Nor is it to say that terrorists never target specific victims. In their campaign of terror in the late 1980s and 1990s, for instance, the Colombian drug cartels assassinated more than 1,000 public officials, including numerous judges and four presidential candidates, in order to intimidate Colombia's entire legal and political system.

In the bombing of Pan Am Flight 103, several groups with grudges against the United States were implicated. That foul play was involved became obvious within a few days to the Federal Bureau of Investi-

gation (FBI) and to the British and Scottish officials who were also investigating the crash. Part of the strategy in any aviation disaster is to recover as many pieces of the wreckage as possible and put the aircraft back together, because this can provide valuable clues to what happened. At Lockerbie a piece of the inside of the aircraft was recovered that showed the pitting and indentations that are characteristic of an explosion.

Investigators knew that in the weeks before the incident, there had been several warnings that Arab

The aftermath of a 1985 machine-gun attack on Rome's Fiumicino Airport, which claimed the lives of 14 travelers. Airports, subways, and train stations have been frequent targets of terrorists, in part because they contain many potential victims in confined spaces.

terrorists were planning to attack an American airplane. The reports had been vague and contained too little information to pinpoint any specific plane, however. Now the FBI began a search among its contacts in the Arab world, eventually enlisting help from the Central Intelligence Agency (CIA), MI6 (the British counterpart of the CIA), Interpol (a European-based international police organization), and the intelligence services of the German, Swedish, Swiss, French, and Maltese governments.

Meanwhile, hundreds of police continued to comb the crash site on their hands and knees in search of even the tiniest scrap of the plane or its cargo. One small piece that was found was a twisted metal plaque that had been inside the passenger luggage area. The condition of the plaque told investigators that the explosion had happened in that compartment. The plaque contained a piece of yellow plastic about the size of a penny. When investigators examined it under a microscope, they discovered that it had been part of a computer chip used in a Toshiba "Bombeat" radio cassette recorder.

Several weeks before the Lockerbie disaster, two members of the Popular Front for the Liberation of Palestine–General Command (PFLP-GC), an extremely radical Palestinian group supported and perhaps even directed by Syria, had been arrested in Frankfurt, Germany. In their possession were Toshiba "Bombeat" radios that had been packed with explosives. Frankfurt was also the city where Flight 103 had originated. Based on these connections, the FBI initiated an intensive but ultimately unsuccessful attempt to apprehend Ahmed Jibril, the leader of the PFLP-GC. Because the Iranian government was also known to support the PFLP-GC and because investigators had uncovered a wire transfer of several million dollars between Tehran and a Vienna bank account controlled by Jibril, the FBI was inclined to give credence to rumors that the

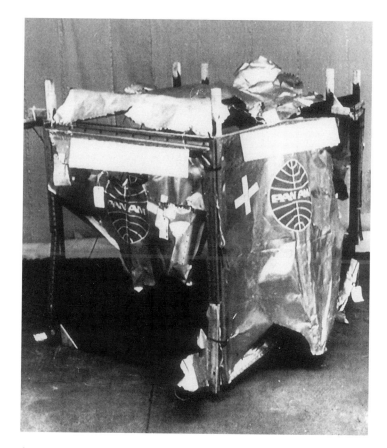

A reconstructed cargo container from Pan Am Flight 103. From the condition of the metal, investigators knew that a bomb had exploded inside this container.

bombing had been financed by the Iranian government. The presumed motive was retaliation.

The previous July, the USS *Vincennes*, patrolling the waters of the Persian Gulf, had shot down an Iranian passenger jet with a surface-to-air missile, killing all 290 Iranian civilians on board. Iran and its neighbor Iraq had been fighting a long and bitter war, and earlier an Iraqi fighter plane had mistakenly fired a missile at another U.S. warship, the *Stark*, killing a number of American sailors. The crew of the *Vincennes*, guarding against a repeat of that incident, misread the radar data on the Iranian airliner and believed it to be a fighter jet in a threatening posture.

Other clues in the Lockerbie case surfaced as the investigation proceeded. It was determined that the

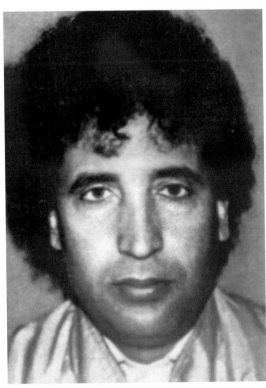

Abdel Basset al-Megrahi (right) and Lamen Khalifa Fhimah, suspects in the bombing of Pan Am Flight 103.

explosion had happened in the part of the baggage compartment reserved for luggage that was put aboard before the plane reached Heathrow Airport. The remnants of a brown Samsonite suitcase revealed that the bomb had been inside it. A tiny sliver of an electronic printed circuit board was found embedded in the fabric of a shirt that investigators believed was inside the suitcase. The sliver appeared identical to a circuit board that had been used in a terrorist attack in the West African nation of Senegal. When that board had been treated with chemicals and then viewed under laser light, investigators discovered that it had been manufactured by a company in Zurich, Switzerland. Discreet inquiries determined that the Swiss company had manufactured 20 prototype digital timers, Model MST-13, for the Libyan government. The timers were capable of initiating an explosion.

Painstaking analysis of scraps of fabric from the suitcase that contained the bomb revealed that the fabrics came from manufacturers in Italy and Malta. Incredibly, it was then determined that the combination of fabrics found could only have come from Mary's House, a small boutique in Sliema, Malta. The shopkeeper at Mary's, Tony Gauci, remembered the man who had bought the particular mix of articles that contained the different fabrics. He even remembered the day, December 7, 1988. Gauci knew that the man was a Libyan because there were many Libyans in Malta and their accents were unmistakable. Using the description Gauci gave the FBI, the CIA compiled photographs of known terrorists who might be the man. From these Gauci picked out Abdel Basset al-Megrahi.

The FBI then traced al-Megrahi's movements in the days preceding the bombing. He had been registered at the Holiday Inn in Sliema on December 7, the day someone fitting his description bought the clothes in question from Mary's House. Two days later, December 9, he had flown to Zurich. On December 17, al-Megrahi flew back to Luqa Airport on Malta and then on to Tripoli, Libya. On December 20, he flew back to Luqa Airport carrying a brown Samsonite suitcase. At 9:50 the next morning, the suitcase was put aboard an Air Malta flight to Frankfurt, Germany, with tags that said "RUSH JFK." Thirty minutes later al-Megrahi took a flight back to Tripoli. Authorities never explained how an unaccompanied suitcase got through the security procedures at two major airports, Frankfurt and Heathrow, that were under notice of a possible terrorist attack. It was rumored that the suitcase had been inserted into a stream of suitcases bound for the United States as part of a heroin-smuggling operation of the Syrian government.

The bombing of Flight 103 is a good illustration of how difficult it can be to get to the bottom of a terrorist incident, when the shadowy organizations and faceless

IN REMEMBRANCE OF ALL VICTIMS
OF LOCKERBIE AIR DISASTER
WHO DIED ON 21st DECEMBER 1988

FRANK CIULLA	WILLIAM DAVID GIEBLER	ALEXANDER LOWENSTEIN	SARAH SUZANNAH BUCHANAN PHILIPPS	PA
THEODORA EUGENIA COHEN	ANDREW CHRISTOPHER GILLIES-WRIGHT	LLOYD DAVID LUDLOW	FREDERICK SANDFORD PHILLIPS	RO
ERIC MICHAEL COKER	OLIVE LEONORA GORDON	MARIA THERESIA LURBKE	JAMES ANDREW CAMPBELL PITT	GE
JASON MICHAEL COKER	LINDA SUSAN GORDON-GORGACZ	JAMES BRUCE MacQUARRIE	DAVID PLATT	HA
GARY LEONARD COLASANTI	ANNE MADELENE GORGACZ	WILLIAM JOHN McALLISTER	WALTER LEONARD PORTER	JO
BRIDGET CONCANNON	LORETTA ANNE GORGACZ	DANIEL EMMET McCARTHY	PAMELA LYNN POSEN	RAC
SEAN CONCANNON	DAVID GOULD	ROBERT EUGENE McCOLLUM	WILLIAM PUGH	CHA
THOMAS CONCANNON	ANDRE NIKOLAI GUEVORGIAN	CHARLES DENNIS McKEE	CRISOSTOMO ESTRELLA QUIGUYAN	MIC
TRACEY JANE CORNER	NICOLA JANE HALL	BERNARD JOSEPH McLAUGHLIN	RAJESH TARSIS PRISKEL RAMSES	STA
SCOTT CORY	LORRAINE FRANCES HALSCH	LILIBETH TOBILA MACALOLOOY	ANMOL RATTAN	JAM
WILLIS LARRY COURSEY	LYNNE CAROL HARTUNIAN	WILLIAM EDWARD MACK	GARIMA RATTAN	ELIA
PATRICIA MARY COYLE	ANTHONY LA	DOUGLAS EUGENE MALICOTE	SURUCHI RATTAN	ANT
JOHN BINNING CUMM	ORA HEN	WENDY GAY MALICOTE	ANITA LYNN REEVES	FLOR
JOSEPH PATRICK C	MAURICE	ELIZABETH LILLIAN MAREK	MARK ALAN REIN	MAR
WILLIAM ALLAN DA	PAMELA	LOUIS ANTHONY MARENGO	JOCELYN REINA	HIDE
GRETCHEN JOYCE	RODNEY	NOEL GEORGE MARTIN	DIANE MARIE RENCEVICZ	ANDF
SHANNON DAVIS	ALFRED	DIANE MARIE MASLOWSKI	LOUISE ANN ROGERS	ARVA
GABRIEL	HE	JANE SUSAN MELBER	EDINA ROLLER	JONA
OM DIKS	R	JOHN MERRILL	JANOS GABOR ROLLER	LAWAI
SHANT		SUZANNE MARIE MIAZGA	ZSUZSANA ROLLER	TOMA
JOYCE C		JOSEPH KENNETH MILLER	HANNE MARIA ROOT	MARK
GIANFRAI		JEWEL COURTNEY MITCHELL	SAUL MARK ROSEN	DAVID
PETER TH		RICHARD PAUL MONETTI	ANDREA VICTORIA ROSENTHAL	ALEXA
DAVID SCO		JANE ANN MORGAN	DANIEL PETER ROSENTHAL	BARRY
MICHAEL J		EVA INGEBORG MORSON	MYRA JOSEPHINE ROYAL	ASAAD
EDGAR HO		HELGA RACHAEL MOSEY	ARNAUD DAVID RUBIN	MRIJIT
SIV ULLA EN		INGRID ELISABETH MULROY	ELYSE JEANNE SARACENI	NICHOL
TURHAN ERC		JOHN MULROY	SCOTT CHRISTOPHER SAUNDERS	PETER
CHARLES TH		SEAN KEVIN MULROY	THERESA ELIZABETH JANE SAUNDERS	RAYMOI
JOANNE FLA		MARY GERALDINE MURPHY	JOHANNES OTTO SCHAUBLE	JANINA
KATHLEEN		SEAN AITKEN MURRAY	ROBERT THOMAS SCHLAGETER	THOMAS
THOMAS BF		KAREN ELIZABETH NOONAN	THOMAS BRITTON SCHULTZ	KESHA
CLAYTON LE		DANIEL EMMETT O'CONNOR	SALLY ELIZABETH SCOTT	JEROME
JOHN PATRI		MARY DENICE O'NEILL	AMY ELIZABETH SHAPIRO	JONATH
ARTHUR FC		ANNE LINDSEY OTENASEK	MRIDULA SHASTRI	
ROBERT GI		BRYONY ELISE OWEN		
TACIE DE				

Two women gaze at the name of a loved one on Lockerbie's memorial to the victims of the Flight 103 bombing. Libya's refusal to turn over the suspects for trial frustrated the victims' families and exposed the limits of Western power in dealing with international terrorism.

perpetrators of the crime may have motivations different from those of their government sponsors. At one time, Ahmed Jibril, the PFLP-GC, and the governments of Syria, Iran, and Libya were all implicated in the bombing. The case of Flight 103 also shows, painfully, that identifying the suspects and gathering a wealth of evidence doesn't necessarily mean that justice will ever be done. On November 14, 1991, after three years of painstaking investigation, al-Megrahi and an accomplice were indicted for the attack, and arrest warrants were issued. But the government of Libya, which itself had had confrontations with the United States over the issue of terrorism, was harboring the men and refused to hand them over to American or international authorities to face trial for the bombing. As of spring 1998, no one had been brought to justice for the killing of 270 innocent civilians.

Like the Lockerbie attack, much of the terrorism that affects American interests today originates in the intractable conflicts of the Middle East, a strategically vital region of the globe where, 2,000 years ago, the seeds of terrorism were first sown.

ANCIENT SEEDS, BITTER HARVEST

In 168 B.C. the Jews in Palestine, the Eastern Mediterranean region that is today divided among Israel, Jordan, and Syria, revolted against the Syrian overlords in their local towns. Called the Maccabean Revolt, this uprising rallied the Jews around the religious concept of uniting all of those who were "zealous for the Torah," the first five books of the Bible and the symbol of Judaism, against foreign gods and foreign political control. When the Romans conquered the region about 100 years later, they installed Herod as king in place of the Jewish Maccabean princes who had ruled since the Syrians had been ousted. Not only was Herod a foreigner, an Idumean, but he also proved to be a cruel and oppressive tyrant. He quickly earned the hatred of the majority of the local Jewish people. Early in his reign, Herod executed Hezekiah, a local chieftain who opposed his tyranny. Hezekiah's son, Judas of Galilee, rose up in revolt in A.D. 6. He called his men "Zealots," harking back to the zealous

Dead and dying Zealots, Jews who, between A.D. 6 and 66, carried out the first recorded terrorist campaign.

Ultimately the decision to abandon terrorism and confront their Roman enemies in traditional military combat proved the Zealots' downfall. This scene depicts the Romans' destruction of Jerusalem in A.D. 70.

Maccabeans a century before. Judas proclaimed God the sole ruler of the Jewish people and demanded that the Jews not cooperate with a Roman census of their people, the same census that caused Joseph and Mary to travel to Bethlehem, where Jesus Christ was born. The Zealots opposed not only the Greek and Roman foreigners who imposed their rule and taxes on the land, but also the local Jewish population that cooperated with their oppressors. The Roman legions who were garrisoned in the Near East were far too powerful to attack directly, and so the Zealots started their revolt with single acts of terror.

The terrorist arm of the Zealots was called the

sicarii, or "dagger-men." According to the historian Flavius Josephus, they were not simply thieves and murderers but religious fanatics who viewed martyrdom, dying in the struggle for their beliefs, as something joyous and desirable. "Their favorite trick," he wrote,

> was to mingle with festival crowds, concealing under their garments small daggers with which they stabbed their opponents. When their victims fell the assassins melted into the indignant crowd, and through their plausibility entirely defied detection. First to have his throat cut by them was Jonathan the high priest, and after him many were murdered every day. More terrible than the crimes themselves was the fear they aroused, every man as in war hourly expecting death.

The Zealots also carried on a widespread program of sabotage. They destroyed the house of the high priest, Ananias, and the palaces of the family of Herod. They burned the public archives to destroy the tax rolls and business records of the province. They burned granaries and sabotaged the water supply of Jerusalem.

The Romans crucified over 2,000 suspected Zealots but failed to stamp out the revolt, which continued underground for the next 60 years, first under Judas and then later his sons, Simeon, Jacob, and Menahem. The conflict grew in intensity and hatred over these years. The brutal repression by Herod and the Romans only drove more of the local population to side with the Zealots. Finally, in A.D. 66, the Zealots felt that they were strong enough to openly confront their Roman rulers. The Zealots then gave up covert terrorist attacks and began overt military operations. It proved a terrible strategic decision. Zealot groups massacred a Roman garrison and occupied the Temple of Jerusalem, but after early Zealot victories, the Romans regrouped and laid siege to Jerusalem, which they took in A.D. 70. The remnants of the Zealots were forced to flee into the countryside, fortifying themselves in various natural strongholds throughout the region. The Romans attacked each of these strongholds in turn and one by one destroyed the Zealots. At the last stronghold, Masada, 960 men, women, and children committed suicide rather than be taken alive.

The Romans continued to track down and execute any Zealots they could find after this. But for the next 60 years, there were sporadic terrorist attacks. Finally, two more open Jewish revolts rocked the Roman rule of the region during the period from 116 to 135, after which the Jews were largely dispersed from Palestine. The Roman emperor Hadrian forbade Jews to enter Jerusalem.

Historically, religion has been at the root of much conflict—and much terrorism—in the Middle East. In the fourth century the Roman emperor Constantine the Great, a convert to Christianity, made Jerusalem a Christian holy city. By the seventh century Arabs fighting under the banner of the newly founded religion of Islam swept out of the Arabian Peninsula and conquered the surrounding regions. Jerusalem, a holy city in the Muslim faith as well, fell in 638. Divisions arose within Islam, however, and two major opposing branches of the religion were established: the Shiites and the Sunnis, branches that still exist today.

Around 1100, Hasan ibn al-Sabbah, the leader of the Ishmaili sect based in Cairo, split from the rest of the Shiites over the question of who should be the new Imam, or Shiite Muslim leader. Hasan took his followers into Sunni Muslim–held territory and established a new state in the Alamut Valley near the Caspian Sea. Soon Hasan commanded a network of mountain strongholds throughout Persia. But the powerful Seljuk Empire—Muslims of Turkish ancestry who ruled the area—wanted to eradicate Hasan's small sect.

Recognizing that his group was no match for the Seljuks in open battle, Hasan planned an extended campaign of terrorism using a small, secret force of fanatical followers. Over the next 150 years this

Shiite Muslim prisoners of war are decapitated by their Sunni enemies. Throughout history, the inability to triumph on the battlefield has been a key factor in a group's decision to adopt a strategy of terrorism. Rarely has that strategy been used more effectively than by the small Ishmaili sect, a Shiite splinter group that kept its powerful enemies at bay for centuries with a cadre of fanatical believers called the Assassins.

force, which drew its strength from a complete devotion to Islam, brought to the region an ever-widening circle of terror.

The Koran, Islam's holy book, contains vivid descriptions of the physical delights that exist in heaven for those who give up their lives in a *jihad*, a holy war against nonbelievers. In an isolated and remote location of his territory, Hasan attempted to re-create this paradise in a magnificent secret garden of delights surrounded by high walls. Before being sent on a terrorist mission, a *fedayee*, or man of sacrifice, would be drugged with hashish and deposited unconscious in the garden of delights, where he'd wake up in the midst of cool springs, fine perfumes, servants, and beautiful women. For a time, he enjoyed himself in this earthly paradise before again being drugged with hashish and sent on his mission—with a vivid dream of the eternal reward that awaited him if he gave up his life. Because they were high on hashish while carrying out their missions, Hasan's terrorists came to be known as the *Hashishi*, or Assassins (from which comes the modern word for someone who murders a politically important figure).

No one who had any connection with the ruling Seljuks was safe. In disguise and armed only with daggers, the Assassins got close to their targets before stabbing them to death in a sacramental act of ritual murder. Hundreds of religious dignitaries, governors of provinces, military officers, and tribal leaders were killed by the terrorists. Particularly frightening to their enemies was the willingness, even joy, with which the Assassins gave up their own lives in their jihad; there really is no defense against such fanatical believers, as 20th-century targets would rediscover in the face of suicide bombers.

Initially based in Persia, the Assassins spread into Syria and, when Christian Europeans launched their own "holy war" against the Muslims, into the biblical Holy Land. The Crusaders, like the Seljuks before them, were enemies of the Ismailis' faith, and the Assassins terrorized them as well. In 1192 an Assassin murdered the Crusader king of Jerusalem, Conrad of Montferrat. Twice Assassins even tried to kill Saladin, the commander of the Muslim forces against the Crusaders. Not until the middle of the 13th century was the power of the Assassins finally destroyed, when a huge Mongol army led by Hulagu, the grandson of Genghis Khan, swept through Persia and Syria.

In their secrecy, religious fanaticism, and joy in martyrdom, the Assassins bear a resemblance to some of the terrorists who have stalked the Middle East, and the rest of the world, in modern times. But, as terror-

ism expert Walter Laqueur points out in his book *The Age of Terrorism*, "contemporary terrorist groups seem to belong to another species altogether." Whereas the Assassins targeted specific individuals, trying to eliminate their enemies one by one, 20th-century terrorists use terrorism as part of a "general systematic strategy" to achieve political goals and tend to favor indiscriminate killing of civilians.

The goal of the modern Palestinian terrorism that has captured the attention of the world and drawn Western nations into the conflict is the establishment of a homeland for Arab Palestinians—and the destruction of Israel. The roots of the struggle are ancient.

After the Jews dispersed from Palestine following the Roman conquest in A.D. 135, they lacked a homeland. Over the centuries, minority Jewish communities

Role reversal: Prime minister Yitzhak Shamir (left) talks with Israeli soldiers after Israel's 1982 invasion of Lebanon to destroy Yasir Arafat's PLO terrorists, who were headquartered in Beirut. Decades before, Shamir had been the terrorist: his Stern Gang had used bombings, assassinations, and sabotage to establish a Jewish homeland.

Swedish diplomat Count Folke Bernadotte (right) with British officers outside the Arab League headquarters in Jerusalem, September 17, 1948. Only hours after this photo was taken, Bernadotte, a United Nations mediator in the Arab-Israeli conflict, was assassinated by the Stern Gang.

were established within the borders of other countries all over the world. After the Turkish Ottoman Empire conquered Palestine in the early 16th century, Jews were again permitted to immigrate to Palestine, where they set up their own settlements alongside the Christian and majority Muslim communities. But Jews throughout the world faced discrimination, persecution, and, especially in eastern Europe, periodic organized massacres, or pogroms. In 1896 the Austrian Jewish journalist Theodor Herzl wrote a brochure in which he declared that the establishment of a Jewish state was the only solution to "the Jewish question." The most appealing site for this state was Palestine, the Jews' original homeland.

The movement to establish a Jewish homeland, called the Zionist movement, gained momentum during the first decades of the 20th century. Before the outbreak of World War I, some 100,000 Jews were living in Palestine. In 1917, in the midst of a successful military campaign against the Ottoman Turks in Palestine, the British issued the Balfour Declaration, which affirmed England's support for the establishment of a Jewish homeland in Palestine, as long as "nothing shall be done which may prejudice the civil and religious rights of existing non-Jewish communities in Palestine."

After the war, the League of Nations granted Great Britain a mandate to administer Palestine. Under the terms of this mandate, "close settlement by Jews on the land" was encouraged. Between 1920 and 1939, approximately 300,000 Jews immigrated to Palestine. Early on, however, conflict arose between the Jews and the Arab Palestinians of the region, who regarded massive Jewish immigration as a threat to their rights.

During the 1920s a Russian-born Jewish immigrant named Vladimir Jabotinsky called for an "iron wall" of violence against the Arabs in Palestine to establish sovereignty over both banks of the Jordan River as the true borders of the Jewish state, Israel. Two Jewish Zionist groups adopted Jabotinsky's message. The Irgun, the "National Military Organization in the Land of Israel," was founded by Menachem Begin in the 1930s. Many years later Begin would become Israel's prime minister. An even more violent group created about the same time was the Stern Gang, led by Yitzhak Shamir, who would also serve as Israel's prime minister. The Stern Gang used systematic terrorist attacks against both the Arabs and the British in the Zionist conflict. Between 1936 and 1939, when an Arab strike protesting British immigration policy regarding Jews led to an armed rebellion, the Stern Gang set off bombs in Arab marketplaces and buses.

To prevent further unrest the British restricted the

number of new Jewish immigrants, but during the Second World War, another 200,000 European Jews, fleeing Nazi Germany's attempt to exterminate them in the gas chambers and concentration camps, were smuggled into Palestine by the Haganah, the Zionist underground in Palestine. Meanwhile, the Irgun and the Stern Gang continued their terrorist campaign, attacking telegraph centers, oil storage depots, British military and police centers, prisons, and roads. British soldiers were randomly murdered in the streets.

In November 1944, the Stern Gang assassinated Lord Moyne, the British resident minister in the Middle East. In July 1946, the Irgun blew up Jerusalem's King David Hotel, the British headquarters in Palestine. Of the 91 people killed in the explosion, 54 were innocent bystanders or employees of the hotel.

Exhausted by World War II and facing a surge of nationalism in its many overseas possessions, Great Britain was willing to abandon its mandate to administer Palestine. The newly formed United Nations decided to partition Palestine into Jewish and Muslim sectors. Israel proclaimed its independence on May 14, 1948, but radical Palestinians refused to accept partition, and the neighboring Arab nations of Egypt, Jordan, Syria, Iraq, and Lebanon immediately declared war on the new Jewish state. The UN sent a special mediator, Count Folke Bernadotte, to negotiate an end to the conflict. When the count publicly expressed concern about the Israeli treatment of Arabs, the Stern Gang assassinated him.

The Israeli military soon got the upper hand in the conflict, and the Irgun and Stern Gang played a paramilitary role in the fighting. They conducted terrorist attacks on Arab villages both inside and outside Israel's territorial borders. They killed or drove off the inhabitants from land wanted for strategic defense or later settlement. For example, on April 9, 1948, the Irgun and the Stern Gang invaded the Arab village of Deir

Yassin near Tel Aviv, shot two-thirds of the villagers, and drove the rest into the countryside.

When the war ended early in 1949, the borders of Israel had been increased to include 77 percent of the old Palestine. Now it was the Arab Palestinians who had no homeland: of the 1.3 million Arabs who had formerly resided in this area, 900,000 had been driven off, the majority ending up in refugee camps in Arab nations such as Jordan.

Terrorism had played an important role in the establishment of Israel. To the displaced Palestinians it seemed to hold promise for winning back their land. By the 1950s a handful of Palestinian resistance groups had organized and had begun to carry out small-scale attacks in Israel. In 1964 the Palestine Liberation Organization (PLO) was formed in Egypt to unite the various Palestinian groups, the largest of which was

PLO chairman Yasir Arafat speaks to a crowd of Palestinian demonstrators in Amman, Jordan, August 1970. Within a month tensions between the PLO and the Jordanian government would flare into war, leading to the expulsion of Arafat and his fighters.

called al-Fatah. The PLO's stated goal was to destroy Israel and establish a Palestinian state. Funding was to come from the oil-rich Arab nations—which, significantly, did not have identical foreign-policy interests and often supported different factions within the PLO.

Early PLO operations included shelling Israeli settlements and infiltrating small bands of commandos into Israel to carry out sabotage or attack civilian targets. But the terrorists found it difficult to strike inside Israel because of the effectiveness of Israeli security measures and the relative absence of Palestinian inhabitants who could provide support and shelter. Plus, Israel's willingness to launch air strikes outside its borders made Palestinian bases vulnerable.

In 1967 the armies of Egypt, Syria, and Jordan prepared for a massive invasion of Israel. But Israel launched a preemptive attack and in the resulting Six-Day War decisively defeated its enemies. As a result of its victory Israel extended its control to East Jerusalem and the West Bank of the Jordan River (previously Jordanian territory), the Gaza Strip and the Sinai Peninsula (formerly belonging to Egypt), and the Golan Heights (formerly Syria's). These territories provided a strategic buffer against Israel's Arab neighbors. However, as the Israelis eventually learned, the occupied territories would not come without a price: from the heavily populated West Bank and Gaza Strip emerged large numbers of embittered Arabs willing to take up the Palestinian cause through acts of terrorism.

By 1969 the Fatah group had gained control of the PLO, and its leader, Yasir Arafat, was named chairman of the PLO's executive committee. From his headquarters in Jordan, Arafat ordered an intensified campaign against Israel, and the PLO stepped up its attempts to infiltrate Israel with commando groups and attack Israeli settlements. But many, if not most, of the attempted attacks on Israel were thwarted, and the Israelis' policy of retaliating with fierce air strikes caused Jordan's King Hussein to try to restrict Palestinian operations launched from within his borders.

Because of the large numbers of Palestinian refugees, the PLO never lacked fighters. And because of its wealthy Arab sponsors, the organization was able to equip and train these fighters and even to obtain heavy weapons such as tanks. But the PLO's brigades were almost useless in fighting their sworn enemy because a direct military attack against Israel would have been suicidal, and terrorist operations required only small squads. In reality, the PLO's army-in-exile had little to do. And despite its vitriolic anti-Israel rhetoric, Arafat's Fatah seemed in no hurry to undertake anything rash, content with its status as a virtual state within a state in Jordan.

But not all Palestinians were happy with the status quo. Abu Daoud, who commanded a force of nearly 15,000 Palestinian fighters in Amman's Wahdat refugee camp, advocated a military strike against King Hussein. Finally the king decided to act. In September 1970 the Jordanian army launched a bitter war against the PLO. By the following July, Arafat and his group had been forced to withdraw completely from Jordan. Many radical Palestinians would fault Arafat for giving up and running—some groups had fought the Jordanian troops to the death—and this engendered much resentment against Fatah and significant rejection of Arafat's leadership.

Deprived of bases from which to launch raids into Israel, splintered into various factions, and having largely failed to capture the notice—much less the sympathy—of the world, the Palestinian cause seemed precariously close to failure. But from the ashes of "Black September," when King Hussein decided to rid his country of the PLO, a more militant Palestinian movement would arise, phoenixlike, bursting onto the world stage in a bloodbath no one could ignore.

THE VARIETIES OF MODERN TERRORISM

In the early-morning hours of September 5, 1972, eight men carrying gym bags scaled the fence surrounding Munich's Olympic Village, where athletes from the 122 nations participating in the 17th Summer Games slept. The men were not, as a guard believed, athletes sneaking back to their dorms after curfew.

Removing hand grenades and Kalashnikov assault rifles from their gym bags, they made their way toward the dormitories where members of the Israeli weight-lifting and wrestling teams slept, and knocked on the door. It was opened by the wrestling coach, Moshe Weinberg, who managed to shout out a warning before the terrorists shot him dead. As the gunmen rushed into the dormitory and kicked open bedroom doors, terrified Israeli athletes jumped out windows, with the terrorists firing at them as they fled. In addition to Weinberg, the wrestling coach, the terrorists killed one Israeli athlete and took nine others hostage.

Within a few hours, the terrorists, their faces concealed behind dark ski masks, appeared before TV cameras to tell the shocked world who they were and what they wanted. They identified themselves as members of a Palestinian organization called Black September, and unless 200 Palestinian prisoners held in Israel and Germany were released, they declared, they would begin killing their Israeli hostages. They also demanded a commercial jet to fly them to a friendly Arab country.

After several hours of negotiations, the West German government informed the terrorists that it—and Israel—would accede to their demands. As evening fell, the eight terrorists and their nine hostages were flown aboard two helicopters to a nearby NATO base, where a fueled Lufthansa airliner awaited. The Germans, however, had no intention of releasing the Palestinian prisoners or allowing the Black September gunmen to escape. They had posted five snipers around the runway perimeter, and as the terrorists left the helicopters to inspect the jet, the snipers opened fire. But only three terrorists were hit, and a 15-minute firefight ensued before the terrorists were pinned down. After about an hour, German tanks drove onto the runway and approached the still-waiting jet and the terrorists. Realizing that all was lost, the terrorists threw hand grenades into one of the helicopters. It exploded and ignited the second helicopter as the tanks opened fire. Nine hostages, five terrorists, and one German policeman were killed.

Although they failed in their stated goal—obtaining the release of their comrades—and although their entire squad was killed or captured, the Black September terrorists succeeded beyond their wildest dreams in a more important mission: publicizing the Palestinian cause. As many as half a billion people around the world watched the unfolding events on live television. Never again would the plight of Arab Palestinians be unknown. As George Habash, the leader of the Popu-

lar Front for the Liberation of Palestine (PFLP), a Marxist group, said in an interview with the Beirut newspaper *Alk-Sayad:*

> The choice of the Olympics, from the purely propagandist viewpoint, was 100 percent successful. It was like painting the name of Palestine on a mountain that can be seen from the four corners of the earth.

Terrorism has always relied on publicity to achieve maximum psychological impact. The ability of, for example, the Assassins to intimidate a Seljuk official stemmed from the official's awareness that others in his position had already been murdered and that he too might be a target. But the Munich attack didn't really seek to create fear; it was primarily propaganda, symbolic—if bloody and ruthless—theater staged for media consumers in the TV age.

It wasn't the first time media-savvy terrorists planned their activities around the press coverage, nor

A hooded terrorist outside the dormitory where members of the Black September group held nine Israeli athletes hostage during the 1972 Munich Summer Olympics. Up to 500 million people worldwide watched the unfolding crisis on television.

would it be the last. But from the terrorists' point of view, it was arguably the most successful. The year before, terrorists had hijacked several jumbo jets to Jordan's Dawson Field and, after releasing all the passengers, blown up two of the planes on the tarmac while the cameras rolled. The explosions made for compelling television, and several other hijackers used on-ground airplane detonations before the novelty wore off.

Terrorists of all stripes quickly learned how to use the media, especially TV. The media, for their part, found it impossible to ignore a story about terrorism, especially when a terrorist leader made himself available for an interview or an incident such as a hijacking promised to provide dramatic images. Critics have often assailed the media for giving a platform to ruthless fanatics. They also say that excessive media coverage inflates the significance of terrorist organizations, so that a small group is made to seem large and powerful by virtue of the abundant coverage.

Journalists counter that their only duty is to report significant events impartially, and terrorism certainly qualifies as significant. (They might also add that terrorism sells newspapers and boosts TV ratings.) Yet at times journalists have seemed to cross the line between impartial reporting and encouraging or even aiding terrorists, sometimes with dire consequences.

In 1974 terrorists murdered a German businessman aboard a hijacked British Airways jet when they learned from the news media that authorities weren't considering their demands but were organizing a rescue mission. The same fate befell a Lufthansa pilot whose plane had been hijacked to Mogadishu, Somalia.

Then there is the strange case of TWA Flight 847, hijacked to Beirut, Lebanon, while en route from Athens to Rome on June 14, 1985. The Shiite hijackers killed a U.S. Navy diver, Robert Stethem, and dumped his body onto the tarmac. Still holding 39 other Americans hostage, they issued their demand:

that Israel release more than 700 Shiite Muslim prisoners it was holding. A few days later, the hijackers transferred custody of the hostages to Amal, the most powerful Shiite militia in Lebanon. The hostage drama would play out over the course of two weeks, and American TV networks moved to ensure that they would get the pictures. The networks reportedly paid Amal $1 million per week for exclusive access. ABC is said to have paid the militia an additional $30,000 for hostage "interview" tapes (on which the hostages, not surprisingly, said their captors were treating them well, statements several hostages would later recant). And, after Israel released 31 of its Shiite prisoners, ABC reportedly paid $50,000 for the right to cover the "farewell banquet" Amal gave for its hostages, who were released on June 30. Throughout the crisis, Walter Laqueur reports, the networks had all devoted at least two-thirds of their nightly news to the story, and on four nights ABC had allotted less than two minutes to all nonhostage news.

Another hostage situation in Lebanon would occupy the attention of the American media—and provide *years* of publicity to a terrorist group. During the 1980s the Islamic Jihad, an Iranian-sponsored Shiite group, kidnapped and held a handful of hostages—Americans, British, French, and, briefly, Soviets—in Beirut. Several of the hostages, including a CIA employee and a Soviet diplomat, were murdered. Islamic Jihad kept the hostages in the news by periodically setting one free and by releasing images or tapes of the men pleading for their freedom or sympathizing with their captors' cause. Aside from the propaganda value of the Western hostages, the terrorists wanted to swap them for Shiite prisoners. That option was publicly rejected because giving in to the terrorists' demands, it was felt, would merely encourage more hostage taking. But behind the scenes, concern for the half-dozen American hostages—fueled by abundant media coverage of their

plight—actually came to drive U.S. policy. In one component of the so-called Iran-contra scandal that rocked the administration of President Ronald Reagan, the U.S. government secretly arranged arms sales to Iran, an enemy of the United States, in the hopes that it would use its influence with Islamic Jihad to secure the release of the hostages.

Though terrorists have become adept at manipulating the media, coverage of a bombing or a hijacking or a murder almost never leads to widespread sympathy

The media and the message: for maximum impact, terrorists seek to reach the largest possible audience, and that generally involves providing news organizations with compelling stories and images. At left: Terrorists blow up an empty jumbo jet at Jordan's Dawson Field while the cameras roll. Above: The Islamic Jihad, which held American hostages in Beirut, released this photo to keep its cause in the news.

for the terrorists' agenda. On the contrary, the public is likely to be outraged. But by and large terrorists don't aim to win public approval (although some terrorists hope to gain prestige among their countrymen by targeting assets or citizens of a hated foreign power, such as the United States). Generalizing about the ideas and aims of terrorists is of dubious merit, however, as each terrorist group or movement arises from unique circumstances and operates in a unique environment. Politically, terrorists may be left-wing or right-wing, and even the intuitive notion that terrorists must be fighting the status quo doesn't always hold. In the 1980s in the Central American nations of Guatemala and El Salvador, for example, "death squads" abducted and murdered thousands of government critics and other people suspected of harboring leftist sympathies in order to stave off political and social change. The Montoneros of Argentina used terrorism in support of Peronism, the Fascist ideology inspired by the Argentine dictator Juan Peron.

Nonetheless, for the purposes of clarity, modern terrorism can be divided into several broad—and imperfect—categories. One category might be called revolutionary terrorism. Terrorists in this category seek to overthrow a government they view as oppressive or illegitimate. (Once again, the distinction between terrorist groups and guerrilla movements should be kept in mind.) Revolutionary terrorists, who typically work in small cells of up to 10 members each, hope isolated acts of terror will be sufficient to destabilize the government.

The father of modern revolutionary terrorism, according to Walter Laqueur, was the Russian organization Narodnaya Volya (NV), which launched a terror campaign against the autocratic regime of the czar. Between 1878 and 1881 the NV assassinated government officials and attempted to kill the czar himself, first by blowing up a train in which he was traveling and later by detonating a mine in the Romanovs' winter palace. Ultimately, the NV was crushed by Russia's secret police, and the czars would rule Russia for nearly four more decades.

Unlike the NV, the Tupamaros, a Uruguayan terrorist organization of the 1960s and early 1970s, did succeed in destroying the government, with disastrous consequences. Uruguay, South America's most progressive and democratic nation, was in the midst of a growing economic crisis when the Tupamaros began their terrorist campaign. Initially the group shunned bloodshed, largely confining its activities to robbing banks and businesses (and sometimes distributing the money to workers), kidnapping businessmen, and temporarily occupying remote villages. But around 1970 their tactics began to emphasize assassinations and bombings, and the Uruguayan military was called upon to deal with the situation. The army not only crushed the Tupamaros but also seized the government in a coup, and for the next 12 years a brutal military dictatorship ruled Uruguay.

The case of Uruguay and the Tupamaros illustrates several important points. First, revolutionary terrorism isn't always directed at repressive governments; it sometimes occurs in free, democratic societies. This is especially true when the terrorists are motivated by a strong ideology such as Marxism-Leninism. If the only goal is to bring about a Communist system, then actual conditions matter little. For example, the Italian Red Brigades and the West German Baader-Meinhof Gang both terrorized prosperous, democratic societies during the 1970s and early 1980s in the name of Marxism-Leninism. Second, revolutionary terrorists may never enunciate their program for bringing about political reform, social justice, or economic improvements. Indeed, they may not even have such a program. The Tupamaros never detailed what they would do if they came to power in Uruguay; they merely spouted the slogan "The Tupamaros are the people and the people are the Tupamaros." The West German terrorists who succeeded the Baader-Meinhof group ignored ideology and merely said they were engaged in "actionism."

Sometimes religion replaces a secular ideology as the inspiration for revolutionary terrorists. Shiite fundamentalists who reject Western values and want to install an Islamic government in Egypt have been particularly brutal in their terrorist attacks, which in the 1990s have targeted the tourist industry. The bloodiest incident occurred in November 1997, when Egyptian Islamic Group terrorists slaughtered more than 60 people, most of them foreigners, who were visiting the pharaohs' tombs at Luxor.

A second category of modern terrorism might be called nationalist/separatist terrorism. Terrorists in this category are often ethnic or religious minorities in a country or are ruled by a foreign nation, and they seek to establish a homeland for themselves or to gain political independence. The Palestinian terrorists are perhaps the best-known practitioners of this type of terrorism—and of course the Zionist terrorists preceded them—but throughout the 20th century a host of nationalist/separatist terrorist movements have existed all over the world.

Members of the Black Hand, a terrorist group composed of Bosnian Serb nationalists, provided the spark that ignited World War I. In Sarajevo in 1914, the group assassinated Archduke Franz Ferdinand, heir to the throne of Austria-Hungary, which had earlier annexed Bosnia and Hercegovina.

In that same decade, terrorist tactics such as assassinations and hit-and-run shootings against military targets were frequently employed by members of the Irish Republican Army (IRA), which was waging a war for independence from Great Britain. The Anglo-Irish War ended in 1921 with a treaty establishing the Irish Free State as a dominion of the British Empire, with the six-county area of Ulster (Northern Ireland) remaining part of the United Kingdom. Within a year, however, civil war had broken out between those who accepted the treaty and those who insisted on a united, independent Irish republic. By 1924 the Republicans' military force, the IRA, was defeated, but their cause did not die, even when the Republic of Ireland, which was completely independent from Great Britain, was established in 1948. Outbreaks of terrorism, mainly small-scale incursions into Northern Ireland from

across the border and attacks on police stations, arose in the 1950s and '60s.

Over the years, religion has assumed a central role in the Irish conflict. The Republic of Ireland is overwhelmingly Catholic, but Northern Ireland is about 60 percent Protestant. Unification would make the Protestants a minority. Economic, social, and political discrimination spurred a civil rights movement among Northern Ireland's Catholics in the late 1960s, and when Protestant groups met generally peaceful Catholic protests with violence, widespread rioting and mob fighting ensued. In 1969 the British army was called in

Belfast, 1988: A car burns under a Republican mural proclaiming the armed struggle against British rule. Religion has played a central role in Irish terrorism. Earlier on the day this photo was taken, Protestant terrorists had shot into the crowd at an IRA member's funeral, killing three mourners and sparking retaliation by Catholics.

to quell the unrest and protect the Catholics, but the soldiers soon clashed with Catholic mobs, and Irish terrorism entered its bloodiest phase. The IRA planted bombs in England and robbed banks in Ireland, but it had suspended most of its terrorist activities by 1972. However, a much more radical terrorist organization, the Provisional Irish Republican Army, had split from the IRA in December 1969. The Provisionals' terrorist campaign in Northern Ireland included murders of Protestant policemen and civilians, ambushes of British soldiers, mortar attacks on police stations, bombings of Protestant stores and bars, and occasional kidnappings. The Provisionals also struck inside England with bombings, including the infamous Birmingham pub attacks that claimed 21 lives and attacks that shut down London's financial district and targeted the British Houses of Parliament. They also planned assassinations, including an unsuccessful attempt on the life of British prime minister Margaret Thatcher and the successful killing of Lord Mountbatten, the first cousin of the queen of England.

Protestant groups such as the Ulster Volunteer Force (UVF) responded with terrorism of their own. They murdered random Catholic civilians and occasionally Republican leaders, and they bombed Catholic meeting places. The bombing of a Catholic bar in Belfast in 1971 killed 15.

The violence in Northern Ireland peaked in 1972, when 467 people were killed, but members of the Provisional IRA and another splinter group, the Irish National Liberation Army, continued terrorist activities sporadically into 1998, as did the Protestant paramilitary groups, despite an official cease-fire and all-party talks that included the IRA's political arm, Sinn Fein.

In Spain another terrorist group has waged a decades-long separatist campaign. That group is the Euzkadi ta Azkazatuna (ETA), and its members are fighting for a homeland not primarily because of eco-

herri
harmatua
inoiz ez
anpatua

EUSKADI TA ASKATASUNA
E.T.A.

iraultzarako
erakunde
harma

nomic, religious, or political repression but because they want to preserve their language and cultural identity. The ETA is made up of Basques, who live in four mountainous provinces in northern Spain. The Basques are one of Europe's oldest ethnic groups, having existed as a people for perhaps 20,000 years.

The ETA formed in the 1950s after Francisco Franco, Spain's Fascist dictator, tried to eradicate the Basques' national identity by suppressing their language and customs and eliminating their leaders. But ETA terrorism escalated after Franco's death in 1975, when more liberal Spanish governments made major conces-

ETA terrorists during a press conference at a secret location. The ETA, which has carried out a decades-long terrorist campaign to win a separate homeland for the Basque ethnic minority in Spain, numbers only a couple hundred fighters and has little chance of achieving its political goals.

sions to the Basques. Murders, assassinations (including the killing of a prime minister, Carrero Blanco), bombings, and several campaigns to cripple Spain's tourist industry have failed to make the Spanish government grant the ETA's demands for a Basque homeland. And, in fact, the ETA's cause appears hopeless. For one thing, polls show that only 10 to 15 percent of the Basques support ETA terrorism, and estimates have put the group's actual fighters at no more than 200 at any time. In addition, about half the population of the Basque provinces is actually not of Basque origin, and these people would be very unlikely to accept living in a Basque homeland. The Basque culture is slowly disappearing because of demographic factors. Despite the absence of popular support and real prospects for success, however, the ETA is likely to continue its campaign of terrorism because of the fanaticism of its members and the financial support of foreign sponsors such as Libya.

Two other nations that have recently experienced nationalist/separatist terrorism are India and its island neighbor to the southeast, Sri Lanka. In India members of the Sikh religious minority formed a terrorist group known as the Militant Sikhs, whose goal is to establish an independent Sikh state in the northern Punjab region. The Militant Sikhs' most devastating action was the 1985 bombing of an Air India commercial jet, which killed 329 passengers and crew. Sikhs also killed India's prime minister, Indira Gandhi, in 1984, but that was believed to be in revenge for an Indian assault on a Sikh temple, not part of an organized terror campaign. In Sri Lanka in the 1980s, terrorism became a key component of the Liberation Tigers of Tamil Eelam's strategy to create an independent state for the nation's Tamil ethnic minority. Massacres of ethnic-majority Sinhalese civilians were common, and the Tamil Tigers were blamed for the assassination of India's prime minister, Rajiv Gandhi, who was killed at a political rally in 1991 by a suicide bomber.

If revolutionary and nationalist/separatist terrorism are distinguishable by the stated goals of their practitioners—leaving aside the question of whether those goals are even remotely achievable—a third category of terrorism, state-sponsored terrorism, is somewhat murkier. A handful of nations are known to sponsor terrorist groups and in some cases to use those groups as an instrument of foreign policy.

On the morning of October 25, 1983, the terrorist group Islamic Jihad, with support from Iran and Syria, launched two suicide truck bombings in Beirut. One

Shortly before this photo was taken on October 25, 1983, a suicide truck bomber had blown up the barracks of the U.S. Marine peacekeepers stationed in Beirut. Intelligence sources believed the attack was sponsored by Iran and Syria.

truck bomb demolished the U.S. Marine barracks, killing 241 American servicemen as they slept; the other killed 58 French soldiers at their headquarters. The soldiers were part of an international peacekeeping force trying to bring an end to Lebanon's long-running civil war. The motivations of the attacks' sponsors, Iran and Syria, aren't too difficult to divine. Since the overthrow of Iran's dictator, the U.S.-supported Shah Mohammad Reza Pahlavi, by radical Shiites led by the Ayatollah Khomeini, Iran and the United States had been bitter enemies. In fact, Khomeini had publicly called for attacks against the United States, and Iran had held U.S. embassy personnel hostage for 444 days between 1979 and 1981. Syria, for its part, stood to lose the considerable influence it wielded in Lebanon if the civil war ended and a strong and stable Lebanese government emerged.

In other cases, however, it's difficult to see what state sponsorship of terrorism achieves for the sponsoring nation. Why, for example, does the anti-American, Muslim, North African nation of Libya sponsor the Provisional wing of the IRA, a generally pro-American, Catholic organization fighting thousands of miles away? And what did Libya's leader, Muammar Gadhafi, hope to achieve by sponsoring the 1986 bombing of a discotheque in Berlin, West Germany, known to be frequented by American servicemen—if indeed Gadhafi's regime was behind the attack, as intelligence reports indicated? He did not—and could not—ever claim credit for that attack, so the bombing could not increase his prestige among anti-American Arabs, and the killing and maiming of Americans and Germans in Germany served no strategic function.

What might have motivated Gadhafi—and what apparently has motivated some other recent terrorists—is hatred of Western society, and in particular, of the United States. The terrorist act isn't being used to coerce—no political goal is ever enunciated, much less achieved—but rather to punish. A seemingly bottom-less well of contempt for America's policies and values spurs a raging desire to inflict damage upon Americans.

In the scope of his plans for striking out at America, and in the single-mindedness with which he approached his mission, one recent terrorist stands apart from the rest.

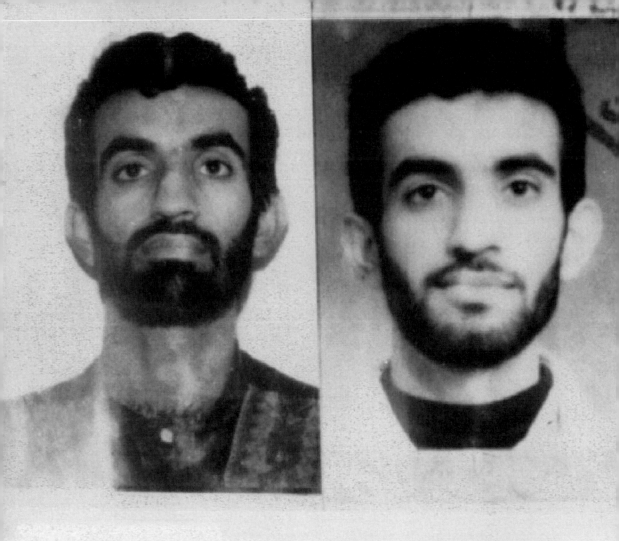

RAMZI AHMED YOUSEF

Date of Birth	May 20, 1967
Place of Birth	Iraq
Race	White
Sex	Male
Eyes	Brown
Hair	Brown
Height	6'0"
Weight	180 pounds
INS A#	A72-054-519

PORTRAIT OF
A TERRORIST

The shadowy mastermind of the 1993 World Trade Center bombing. His real name, date of birth, and place of birth aren't known for certain.

In September 1992, a tall young man in Arab dress tried to enter the United States through the Immigration and Naturalization office at New York City's John F. Kennedy Airport. He bore an identity card in the name of Khurram Khan. When the immigration officer rejected his documents, the young man quickly presented what appeared to be a legitimate Iraqi passport in the name of Ramzi Ahmed Yousef.

Yousef claimed to be a member of a guerrilla group that opposed Saddam Hussein, the Iraqi dictator whose forces a U.S.-led coalition had defeated the year before in the Gulf War. He was known in Iraq, he said. He had been tortured by Hussein's forces and would be shot if the American government repatriated him to Iraq. He sought asylum in the United States.

At the next counter in the immigration office, one of Yousef's traveling companions, Ahmad Ajaj, was having a more difficult time. Ajaj was carrying a fake Swedish passport, and in his luggage officials found bomb-making equipment, videotapes that called for war on the United States and that demonstrated how to bomb buildings, and bomb-making manuals. Ajaj was arrested. Yousef's fingerprints were later found on the manuals in Ajaj's luggage.

As officials surrounded his companion at the next counter, Yousef calmly and convincingly presented his own story to explain away passport irregularities. He was granted political asylum, permitting him to remain in the United States.

Yousef left John F. Kennedy Airport and disappeared into the Muslim community of nearby Jersey City, New Jersey. Jersey City contains a large Arab community, and Yousef quickly found his way into the inner circle of the Al Salam mosque, which was led by a blind Muslim cleric, Sheik Omar Abdel Rahman. Sheik Rahman had come to the United States to avoid arrest in his native Egypt, where he was wanted for his role in assassinations and other terrorist acts.

Ramzi Yousef, perhaps aided explicitly or implicitly by Sheik Rahman, began to enlist Al Salam members to help him carry out the mission he had come to the United States to fulfill: bombing the World Trade Center, New York City's twin 110-story skyscrapers. Within two days of his arrival, Yousef had met and become the roommate of another follower of Sheik Rahman, a young Palestinian named Mohammed Salameh. Yousef and Salameh assumed a common identity, each using the alias Abrahim Kamal over the next few months. They and several other conspirators purchased chemicals that could be used in making a bomb, rented a shed to store the chemicals, and rented an apartment where the fuse could be assembled.

Members of Sheik Rahman's inner circle dreamed of a series of bombings at New York City locales: the Holland and Lincoln tunnels, the United Nations headquarters, the FBI headquarters in lower Manhattan. But, as later events would demonstrate, they were a rather inept bunch. Yousef, on the other hand, intended to carry out just one bombing before fleeing the United States, but it would wreak unimaginable destruction. Yousef hoped his bomb would topple one of the World Trade Center's towers into the other, and, like two huge dominoes, the buildings would crash down on Manhattan's Lower End. According to prosecutors at his trial, Yousef believed that he could cause 250,000 deaths.

Anyone who could attempt the indiscriminate killing of a quarter million people must be a fanatic (or a lunatic), and indeed, the popular conception of terrorists is of ideologues whose blind, burning devotion to a cause leads them to use whatever means necessary—even to sacrifice their own lives—to achieve their ends. While many terrorists do fit this profile, many others don't, and beyond a few generalizations, not much can be said about a "terrorist personality."

Sheik Omar Abdel Rahman, the blind Islamic fundamentalist cleric who was at the center of a plot to bomb several famous New York City landmarks.

Reducing the question of who is a terrorist to its most basic terms, it might be said that terrorists are criminals distinguishable from others who commit similar crimes—murder, extortion, kidnapping, arson—by their different motivations. The common criminal is motivated by factors such as greed, anger, and psychological or social maladjustment; the terrorist, on the other hand, is motivated by principles, regardless of how wrong they may in fact be. But clearly this is an oversimplification and is not always true. For many terrorists money is a more important consideration than

Still standing, the twin towers of the World Trade Center rise above debris from the underground parking garage where a truck bomb exploded. According to prosecutors, the intent of the terrorists had been to topple the towers into Lower Manhattan, killing as many as 250,000 people.

principle.

Abu Nidal (the nom de guerre of Sabri al Banna) began his career with the PLO and may have been a member of the Black September group. But he broke with Yasir Arafat's Fatah faction—supposedly because it wasn't radical enough—and formed his own terrorist group, winning generous financial support, including $15 million worth of weapons and $150,000 a month for operating expenses, from the government of Iraq. Iraq also gave Abu Nidal a personal gift of up to $5 million. But the firebrand who faulted Arafat for his too-conservative approach to the Palestinian cause hardly used his newfound resources to lash out at Israel. He was sponsored by Iraq, and he did Iraq's bidding, concentrating his terrorist attacks on Syrian, Jordanian, and PLO targets and several times attempting to kill Arafat. Later he switched allegiances to Syria, and still later to Libya, earning a reputation for selling his services to the highest bidder.

Similar contradictions between practice and principle can be found in the recent phenomenon of narco-terrorism. Since at least the early 1980s terrorists have done important work for drug traffickers in return for money and arms. The terrorists have guarded drug traffickers' airstrips and laboratories, granted them safe passage through territories they controlled, even attacked government (sometimes U.S.) antinarcotics units. Typical of the terrorists' symbiotic relationship with the drug barons is Peru's Sendero Luminoso, or Shining Path. Shining Path, which modeled itself upon the teachings of China's Mao Zedong, earned a reputation for bizarre and brutal acts and for ideological purity. The group once hung dead dogs bearing the message "Those dogs who vote will die like this" on the lampposts of Lima and Ayacucho, hoping to discourage citizens in those cities from voting in elections. In the remote regions where Shining Path concentrated its efforts, the group executed not only policemen and public officials but also prostitutes and gamblers, whom they called parasites. Shining Path initially took a dim view of the drug trade as well, fiercely battling the traffickers in the jungles of Peru. At some point, however, pragmatism replaced ideology, and Shining Path began collecting money from the drug traffickers in exchange for protection and safe haven. Similar involvement in the drug trade has been documented among Bolivian, Colombian, Tamil, Armenian, Turkish, and Middle Eastern terrorists.

Drug traffickers have also waged their own terrorist campaigns, most notably in Colombia. In order to stop the government from vigorously prosecuting their members, the notorious Medellín and Cali cocaine cartels assassinated judges and politicians and bombed a wide variety of civilian targets. After it had become clear that Colombia's justice system had been thoroughly intimidated (and corrupted through bribery), the United States pressured the Colombian government into agreeing to extradite (turn over to another government for trial) drug kingpins to the United States. Calling themselves the Extraditables, a group of cartel members announced a terrorist war against Colombian society. The Colombian constitution was soon amended to prohibit extradition to foreign nations.

Although its goals aren't often so purely criminal, to a certain extent terrorism has always been a Machiavellian enterprise: in the terrorist's view, the ends sought (which are generally expressed as the attainment of a more equitable or just society) justify the means (which often include the killing of innocent civilians). But according to terrorism expert Walter Laqueur, terrorists in recent decades have become much more ruthless. The Russian terrorists who tried to overthrow the czar in the 1880s agonized over the morality of killing czarist officials. Even as late as the 1930s, the indiscriminate killing of civilians wasn't recognized as an appropriate tactic. Now, Laqueur says, "[k]illing without hesitation, often without thought and reason, has become the rule, and, at least to some of the murderers, the act of killing has been a source of thrills and enjoyment."

No one but Ramzi Ahmed Yousef can say whether the idea of killing hundreds of thousands of people in Manhattan was a source of thrills and enjoyment for him. At his trial, Yousef claimed to be fighting for the Palestinian cause and declared his hatred for the United States, but very little is definitively known about him. Even the name Ramzi Yousef is almost certainly an alias.

Like most terrorists, Yousef was young (in his mid-twenties) when he carried out his terrorist acts. (That the majority of terrorists are young is probably not too surprising, as the life of a terrorist is dangerous and incompatible with a settled lifestyle.) He seems to have received a good education and to have traveled widely, and experts believe he was at one time educated in England. He speaks English, Arabic, and Urdu, an official language of Pakistan, fluently and may know several other languages as well. Studies have shown that most terrorists are educated and come from middle- or upper-middle-class backgrounds. Often they are the children of professionals such as doctors, lawyers, and government officials. This, however, is true only of the majority of terrorist groups; IRA membership, for

example, comes almost exclusively from the working class. Women as well as men are found among the ranks of terrorists, though again, that depends upon the specific terrorist organization. The Basque ETA, for example, has always shunned participation by women, but in other groups, such as the Italian Red Brigades and the German Baader-Meinhof Gang, women have actually constituted a majority.

According to some sources, Yousef is a native Kuwaiti or Iraqi who was living in Peshawar, Pakistan, during the 1980s, when American arms were being funneled through Pakistan to the mujahedin, Afghan Muslim guerrillas fighting to oust Soviet troops from their country. Yousef may have learned the rudiments of bomb making from mujahedin using Pakistan as a training base; he may even have learned about explosives from the CIA, which was active in training

Colombian soldiers move to seal off the site of a bombing by the Medellín cocaine cartel. The drug barons' campaign of bombings, assassinations, and murders—along with their use of bribery—was so successful in intimidating and corrupting Colombia's government and legal system that some observers now call the South American nation a "narco-democracy."

Afghan fighters. According to some linguistics experts at the FBI, Yousef is a Palestinian, probably from Jordan; Israeli intelligence sources say he's probably from the occupied West Bank. Still another FBI profile listed him as a Pakistani born in Kuwait. In a 1994 interview with an Arabic newspaper, Yousef said his father was Pakistani and his mother Palestinian, and his real name is Abdul-Basit Balochi. To his neighbors in Jersey City, however, he was known simply as "Rashid the Iraqi."

Whatever his origins, Yousef proved a much more resourceful and elusive terrorist than the Al Salam mosque members whom he enlisted in the World Trade Center bombing plot. Several weeks before the bombing was to occur, Yousef went to the Pakistani consulate and, in fluent Urdu, convinced officials that he was a Pakistani named Abdul Basit who had been born in Kuwait in 1968. He was granted a Pakistani passport.

On February 26, 1993, Yousef and another conspirator, Eyad Ismoil, drove a van that Yousef's roommate, Mohammed Salameh, had rented from the Ryder Truck Rental Company into the parking garage beneath the World Trade Center. They parked, got into another car, and drove away. Inside the van was a homemade 1,200-pound urea-nitrate bomb.

The truck bomb exploded just after noon, but it failed to topple the World Trade Center, which at the time held about 50,000 people in its twin 110-story office buildings, its hotel, and its ground-floor shopping complex. Nevertheless, the bomb did considerable damage, destroying several levels of the parking garage. Six people were killed, more than 1,000 were injured, and the Lower End of Manhattan, including Wall Street, was virtually shut down, resulting in economic losses estimated at $650 million.

Yousef and Ismoil left their Al Salam companions to their fate. Within 11 hours of the blast, Yousef had departed John F. Kennedy Airport on board a commer-

cial flight to Karachi, Pakistan. He was traveling with his Pakistani passport in the name of Abdul Basit.

Largely because of the ineptitude of some of the conspirators, the FBI was able to solve the World Trade Center bombing fairly quickly. Scorch marks identified the source of the explosion as the van, and the vehicle identification number that every car and truck bears on its chassis enabled investigators to trace the van's registration to Ryder. The company searched its records and found that the van was rented to a Mohammed Salameh, who, incredibly, had returned to the Ryder rental station three hours after the explosion to report the van stolen and ask for his $400 deposit back. The agent had told him that he had to report the theft to police and then return to the agency with a copy of the police report.

Members of Peru's Sendero Luminoso, or Shining Path. Though it initially opposed the narcotics trade as a blight on society, Shining Path and the drug traffickers came to a happy accommodation: in exchange for money and weapons, the terrorists gave the traffickers protection and safe haven.

On March 4, as Salameh walked out of the rental agency with his money, he was arrested. In his shirt pocket was the business card of Nidal Ayyad, a chemical engineer. The two men shared a joint bank account and had rented a car together. Ayyad was soon arrested. When police searched Salameh's apartment, they found tools, wiring diagrams, and books on electronics. They opened the storage shed he was renting and discovered 100-pound bags of urea, as well as bottles of nitric and sulfuric acid, components of the Trade Center bomb.

As the probe widened, two more men with connections to Sheik Rahman were arrested. Because everyone involved seemed to be connected to the sheik, the FBI decided to infiltrate his group with an Egyptian-born informant named Emad Salem, who was able to get a job as Rahman's bodyguard. Salem uncovered plots to bomb other New York City landmarks, and Rahman and nine associates were arrested.

Rahman and these nine followers were convicted in 1995 of conspiring to blow up the United Nations, the FBI's New York headquarters, and the Lincoln and Holland tunnels. The year before, Salameh and three others had been convicted and sentenced to prison terms of 240 years each for the World Trade Center bombing. But prosecutors were well aware that the mastermind of that terrorist attack—the man the other conspirators knew as Rashid the Iraqi—was not present: throughout the trial, a large photo of Yousef stood in the courtroom, and the prosecution referred to him as the "evil genius" behind the bombing.

As the CIA and the FBI conducted a massive intelligence-gathering effort to learn his whereabouts, Ramzi Yousef was planning more terrorist attacks. But for a year and a half, the American agencies found very little information. Some of that time, it appeared later, Yousef spent in Pakistan, where he is believed to have associated with students at Islamabad International Islamic University, which has a fundamentalist Islamic

philosophy. It is safe to assume that Yousef had at least some university training himself. Several studies have shown that worldwide, over half the terrorists have a university degree or, in the United States, some university training. Yousef, a terrorist as well as a student, was soon in operation again. He went to the Philippines, a country with an active fundamentalist Islamic revolution on its southern islands, and began to recruit terrorist operatives in Manila and Cebu.

On December 9, 1994, Yousef purchased, in the name Armaldo Forlani, a ticket for a Philippine Air Line flight between Manila and Cebu a month later. He specifically requested seat 26 in the economy section. When he got off the plane in Cebu, Yousef left behind a bomb under his seat. Two hours later, as the flight continued on to Tokyo, the bomb exploded. A

A State Department employee displays posters publicizing the $2 million reward being offered for information leading to the arrest of Ramzi Yousef. A tip led to the terrorist's capture in Pakistan in 1995.

Japanese passenger was killed, and the crippled plane was forced to make an emergency landing at Okinawa. The entire operation was thought to be a trial run, a test of the ability of a newly created Philippine terrorist cell to get a bomb aboard an international flight. What Yousef envisioned, according to prosecutors, was a series of larger bombs that would bring down a dozen airliners almost simultaneously over the Pacific, causing 4,000 deaths. He never got the opportunity to carry out this plan.

On January 6, 1995, six days before the planned arrival of Pope John Paul II on the Philippine leg of his Asian tour, Manila police raided room 603 of the Josefa Apartments. The apartment, which overlooked the pope's route into town from the airport, had been rented to a Naji Owaida Haddad. Haddad was the alias Yousef was using; he shared the apartment with his girlfriend, Carol Santiago. Evidently the two were tipped off just before the police raid, because they left supplies and evidence behind. Investigators found bomb-making equipment, a map of the pope's parade route, Bibles, priest's clothing, timing devices, sulfuric acid, and airline schedules for American trans-Pacific flights. Yousef's fingerprints were everywhere.

After fleeing Manila, Yousef and Santiago traveled south into the Muslim-held islands of the Philippines. From there, they escaped to Malaysia. Yousef then traveled to Bangkok, Thailand. Authorities in the United States were informed that Yousef was there, planning a bombing of the Israeli embassy, or maybe a bombing of an American flight out of Bangkok. Neither plan materialized. One informer said that Yousef cancelled the plan against the airplane after reviewing the security measures at the airport.

By February, Yousef apparently needed to renew his supplies or believed that authorities were getting too close. He made plans to return to safe territory, Iran or Iraq. He flew to Islamabad, Pakistan, and was apparently headed for Peshawar, a Pakistani city on the border with Afghanistan. From Afghanistan, he would have easy access to either Iran or Iraq and would have been beyond the reach of Western justice.

But the United States had offered a $2 million reward for information leading to Yousef's capture, and American authorities got a tip that the terrorist was in a hotel in Islamabad. Ten law enforcement agents burst into room 16 of the Holiday Inn's Su Casa Guest House, where they found Yousef, beardless and with his black hair dyed red, lying on the bed. In addition to clothes, his suitcases contained bomb-making equipment, two radio-controlled toy cars packed with explosives, and flight schedules for United and Delta airlines. The agents dragged the screaming man downstairs and threw him into a waiting van, which hustled him off to the airport, where a U.S. military jet was ready to fly him to New York.

In 1996 Yousef was convicted of the Philippine airline bombing that killed a Japanese passenger and of plotting to bomb 12 U.S. airliners. In November 1997 he was convicted of masterminding the World Trade Center bombing. At his sentencing on January 8, 1998, U.S. District Judge Kevin Duffy imposed 240 years in prison without parole for the Trade Center blast and tacked on an additional life term for the airline bombing plot. Reacting to Yousef's claim to be a devout Muslim fundamentalist, Duffy declared, "You adored not Allah but the evil you had become. . . . You just wanted to kill for the thrill of killing human beings."

In a 20-minute presentencing statement, Yousef had been defiant. "Yes, I am a terrorist, and I'm proud of it," he declared. "I support terrorism as long as it is used against the United States and Israel. You are more than terrorists. You are butchers, liars, and hypocrites."

THE ENEMY
WITHIN

At nine o'clock in the morning on April 19, 1995, a little more than two years after Ramzi Yousef and his coconspirators had detonated a truck bomb under New York City's World Trade Center, the people of Oklahoma City were moving to the familiar rhythms of another workday. At the Alfred P. Murrah Federal Building, parents deposited their young children at the day care center, and government workers settled into their daily tasks.

Inside a Ryder rental truck parked in front of the Murrah building was up to 4,000 pounds of ammonium nitrate, a common fertilizer, mixed with 1,000 pounds of fuel oil. At 9:02 A.M. the homemade bomb exploded. "Everything just went black," a witness recalled. "It was like somebody had turned out the lights. And then, it seemed like the whole world ended."

The massive explosion blew off the front of the nine-story building and collapsed one floor upon another, trapping the dead and injured under tons of

71

rubble. For almost two weeks, rescue workers would pull bodies from the ruins, and the death toll eventually reached 168. It was the worst act of terrorism ever to take place on American soil.

In the immediate aftermath of the bombing, reporters and terrorism experts began speculating on who might be responsible for the attack. Which terrorist organizations, they wondered, had the resources to mount an operation of this magnitude in the heartland of America? An early eyewitness report described two men speeding away from the scene as appearing Middle Eastern, so suspicion briefly settled upon Palestinian or Islamic fundamentalist terrorists.

It is perhaps not too surprising that Americans reflexively looked beyond their borders for the perpetrators of the Oklahoma City bombing. After all, terrorists had frequently targeted U.S. citizens abroad—and the only recent large-scale terrorist attack on U.S. soil, the World Trade Center bombing, had been carried out by Arab militants—but there were very few instances of homegrown terrorists striking their fellow Americans.

A significant portion of the American-on-American terrorism in the second half of the 20th century has been committed by Puerto Rican nationalists. The Caribbean island of Puerto Rico was a Spanish possession from the time of Columbus's second voyage in 1493 until 1898, when the United States defeated Spain in the Spanish-American War. According to the terms of the Treaty of Paris, which formally ended the hostilities, Spain ceded Puerto Rico to the United States. After a brief period of military rule, a civil government was established. In 1917 residents of the Puerto Rican colony were made citizens of the United States, although they were not allowed to vote in presidential elections and the island's governor was appointed by the U.S. president. Greater autonomy came after World War II. In 1947 the U.S. Congress granted Puerto Rico

An FBI agent displays weapons and disguises seized after the arrest of four terrorists belonging to the Puerto Rican group FALN. The United States has experienced comparatively little actual terrorism, but a significant portion has been perpetrated by Puerto Rican nationalist groups like the FALN.

the right to elect its own governor; in 1950 it empowered Puerto Ricans to draft a constitution. The resulting document, which took effect in 1952, made Puerto Rico an internally self-governing commonwealth associated with the United States.

Not everyone was satisfied with these arrangements, however. On November 1, 1950, Puerto Rican terrorists seeking total independence for their home-land tried to assassinate President Harry S. Truman. One White House policeman was killed in the incident. On March 1, 1954, Puerto Rican nationalist terrorists opened fire in the U.S. House of Representatives, wounding five congressmen.

After that, several Puerto Rican terrorist groups carried out periodic bombings, in both Puerto Rico and the continental United States. The most prominent of these groups, the Fuerzas Armadas de Liberación Nacional (Armed Forces of National Liberation, better known by its Spanish acronym, FALN), was formed in New York City in 1974 with the goal of establishing an independent, Communist Puerto Rico. Operating in the continental United States, FALN conducted over 150 bombings and acts of sabotage directed primarily at government buildings, corporate offices, and military installations. An FALN bomb in New York City's historic Fraunces Tavern killed four people and injured several dozen more. In 1980 the FBI arrested 13 FALN terrorists, including the group's leader, Carlos Alberto Torres, after which FALN operations in the United States virtually ceased, though they continued for a time in Puerto Rico.

The Macheteros ("Machete Wielders"), another Puerto Rican separatist group, staged a rather spectacu-lar operation in January 1981, blowing up nine jets on the ground at a National Guard base in Puerto Rico. In 1985 the group's effectiveness was seriously hampered by the arrest of 16 of its members. The Organization of Volunteers for the Puerto Rican Revolution (OVRP) is another small terrorist organization active on the island.

The turbulent 1960s and 1970s produced some rev-olutionary terrorism in the United States, mostly from small groups that viewed American society as morally bankrupt, economically unjust, and socially and politi-cally illegitimate. The Weather Underground split off from Students for a Democratic Society (SDS), an organization whose activities included support for the civil rights movement and opposition to the Vietnam War, in 1969. The Weathermen thought that terrorism would catalyze a revolution of students, workers, and African Americans, but beyond that their beliefs were vague and confusing. They orchestrated scores of bombings, mainly directed at what they saw as the twin pillars of injustice, government and capitalist business, and mainly designed to destroy property, although some people were killed. Though they made headlines at the time, the Weathermen had a negligible effect on American society, and with the end of the Vietnam War and a decline in radicalism, they faded away.

Another, even more marginal, revolutionary terrorist group arose in Berkeley, California, and called itself the Symbionese Liberation Army (SLA). According to the SLA, the term *Symbionese* meant "body of harmony of dissimilar bodies and organisms living in deep and loving harmony and partnership in the best interest of within the body"—which may be indicative of the clarity of the group's political agenda. That agenda, insofar as it *was* political and not purely criminal (several of the members were convicts), involved war against the "fascist capitalist class," and relieving banks and businesses of their money was a key tactic. Despite its small size—the "army" comprised fewer than a dozen fighters—the SLA managed to win an enormous amount of publicity when, on February 4, 1974, it kidnapped Patty Hearst, the 19-year-old daughter of newspaper publisher Randolph A. Hearst.

Over the next several weeks, the SLA stayed in the news by periodically releasing to radio stations tapes and letters detailing their demands, one of which was that Randolph Hearst feed all of California's poor (estimated cost: $230 million). Hearst did give away more than $2 million in food, but his daughter's release was not forthcoming. On April 3 events took a strange turn, as the SLA released a tape on which Patty Hearst claimed to have joined the terrorist group. On April 15 she held a submachine gun as the SLA robbed a bank, and a month later she was involved in a shooting at a sporting-goods store. Police ended the bizarre terrorist spree on May 17, when they killed six SLA members in a shoot-out.

Another group that flirted with terrorism during the late 1960s and early 1970s was the Black Panthers. Founded in 1966 by black nationalists Huey Newton and Bobby Seale, the Black Panthers' original mission was to protect African Americans in the ghetto from police abuse and to foster black nationalism. Later the group founded black schools and organized nutrition programs and medical clinics. But a militant faction inspired by Eldridge Cleaver came to shun nonviolent methods and planned a series of bombings of public

Ghosts of racial terror: the Ku Klux Klan.

places. This phase didn't last long, however, and after living in exile in Cuba, Algeria, and North Korea, Cleaver renounced violence.

Another strand of homegrown American terrorism is racist in character and dates back more than a century. In 1866, the year after the Civil War ended, six Confederate veterans living in Pulaski, Tennessee, formed a social club called the Ku Klux Klan. Membership grew rapidly, and chapters were established in many towns throughout the South. Soon the Klan mutated from social club to terrorist organization, and in 1867 Nathan Bedford Forrest, a former Confederate general, took command of the group. The Klan's goal was simple: to maintain white supremacy by intimidating recently freed black slaves. The group's tactics included kidnapping and lynching blacks at night, burning down black schools, and attacking anyone viewed as sympathetic to political equality for blacks.

Strong action by the federal government shattered the Klan by 1872. But by then its terrorist campaign had achieved its goals—namely, preventing African Americans from voting, and maintaining segregation in public places.

The Ku Klux Klan reemerged in several incarnations after its original demise, and terrorism became one of its major tools during the civil rights movement of the 1950s and 1960s. As the courts began to dismantle the South's system of segregation and African Americans demanded—and started to gain—political equality, the Klan moved to intimidate through a campaign of terror. Cross burnings near the homes of African Americans were a common act, meant to symbolize the Klan's power and the target's vulnerability. But Klan terrorism wasn't purely symbolic. Klansmen committed lynchings, bombed African-American homes and churches, burned black-owned businesses, and assaulted nonviolent protesters and civil rights workers. Ultimately, however, this wave of Klan terror-

Bruce Carroll Pierce, a member of the white supremacist group the Order, is taken into custody. In the mid-1980s the Order launched an 18-month terrorist campaign that included bank robberies, synagogue bombings, and murders. Its mission: to establish a whites-only "homeland" in the Northwest.

ism failed to derail the civil rights movement; if anything, widespread revulsion at Klan violence spurred legislative action and accelerated civil rights gains.

Today the Klan exists not as a unified organization but as several dozen distinct groups that share the Klan name but have different leaders and agendas. Despite isolated racial attacks committed by Klansmen, there is no evidence of a Klan-directed campaign of terrorism. However, the most militant members of the Klan have forged links with other white supremacist hate groups. One of these hate groups, the Aryan Nations, was formed by a man named Richard Butler in the 1970s as the Church of Jesus Christ Christian. Headquartered in Hayden Lake, Idaho, the Aryan Nations seeks to establish a whites-only "homeland" comprising the states of Washington, Oregon, Idaho, Montana, and Wyoming. The Aryan Nations earned a reputation as the most violent right-wing group in America, and it boasted rhetoric to match. Police, for example, were called agents of Satan and worthy of assassination, and members could earn "Warrior" status by killing a police officer or government official.

Incredibly, however, Butler's Aryan Nations wasn't violent enough for some white supremacists. During the 1980s several more-militant factions broke off from the parent organization. One of these factions, known variously as the Bruder Schweigen (Silent Brotherhood), White American Bastion, Aryan Resistance Movement, and White American Army of National Liberation for the Aryan Nations—but most familiarly as the Order—launched an antigovernment terrorist campaign in the cause of establishing a white homeland.

The Order's founder, Robert Mathews of Whidby Island, Oregon, was inspired by a 1978 novel called *The Turner Diaries*, written by William Pierce. The book chronicles the successful struggle of a group of fictional white supremacists against a Jewish-controlled federal government. Mathews formed an underground terrorist army along the lines of the fighting force in *The Turner Diaries*.

The Order approached its mission with a religious zeal similar to that of some Muslim terrorists. They believed that whites are God's chosen people, that blacks are subhuman, and that Jews are children of Satan. God, therefore, sanctioned their terrorist activities, they reasoned.

Beginning in 1983, the Order committed a series of bank and armored car robberies to finance its operations; it also had a large counterfeiting operation. Mathews's followers murdered a state trooper and killed a Denver-based radio host, Alan Berg, who had been openly critical of white supremacist groups. The Order also bombed a number of synagogues.

By the fall of 1984, law enforcement had begun to

close in on the terrorists. On October 18 the FBI cornered a faction of the Order in Sandpoint, Idaho; on November 24, there was another confrontation between the FBI and the Order in Portland, Oregon. On December 8 Robert Mathews, the founder of the Order, was killed in a shoot-out with the FBI at his home on Whidby Island. With its leader dead and 24 of its members behind bars, the Order's terrorist activities were effectively ended.

But the hatred of the U.S. government that, along with racism and anti-Semitism, formed the core of the Order's beliefs didn't disappear. When, more than a decade after the death of Robert Mathews, the FBI investigated the bombing of Oklahoma City's Alfred P. Murrah Federal Building, it found that the perpetrators were not foreign terrorists, but a pair of former U.S. Army soldiers with an intense hostility toward the government.

An hour and a half after the Murrah bombing, an Oklahoma Highway Patrol officer arrested Timothy McVeigh, 27, for driving without a license plate. While McVeigh waited in jail, FBI investigators began to piece together what had happened in Oklahoma City. By April 21, two days after the Murrah explosion, they realized that McVeigh might have been involved, and just before he was to have been released for the traffic violation, he was charged in the bombing. The trail soon led to Terry Nichols, a 39-year-old former soldier with whom McVeigh had undergone army basic training.

As investigators dug further, they discovered an apparent motive for the bombing. Both men, it seemed, believed that the federal government had grown tyrannous, repressing unpopular beliefs and violating the rights of citizens, especially the right to bear arms. Particularly infuriating for McVeigh was the FBI's siege of the Waco, Texas, compound of a religious cult known as the Branch Davidians, which began with

charges of weapons violations against the cult. Exactly two years before the Oklahoma City bombing, that siege had ended in a fiery conflagration that claimed the lives of 75 cult members.

Many friends and former associates asserted that McVeigh was an avid reader of *The Turner Diaries* and even sold the book, at a discount, at gun shows. *The Turner Diaries* contains a scene in which white supremacists use an ammonium nitrate bomb to destroy FBI headquarters in Washington, D.C. A similar bomb leveled the Murrah building. According to prosecutors, McVeigh and Nichols targeted the federal building to strike a blow against government tyranny. Of the

Timothy McVeigh, one of two men convicted in the Oklahoma City bombing, apparently wanted to strike a blow against what he viewed as the tyranny of the federal government.

168 people killed in the Oklahoma City bombing, however, only 8 were actually government agents; the
majority merely worked for government agencies, and
19 children also died.

The two men were tried in separate federal trials.
McVeigh was convicted of eight counts of murder, conspiracy to use a weapon of mass destruction, using a
weapon of mass destruction, and destruction of a federal building; he was sentenced to death. Nichols was
convicted of one count of conspiracy and eight counts
of involuntary manslaughter and was sentenced to life
imprisonment.

Aside from shattering Americans' sense of security
from terrorist attacks at home, the Oklahoma City
bombing revealed a right-wing subculture most people
had never heard of: the militia movement. Though it
was never conclusively demonstrated that either
McVeigh or Nichols was an active member of a militia,
their actions, some commentators noted, seemed
inspired by militia rhetoric, or at the very least, their
antigovernment views and those of the militias were
quite similar.

The central concern of the militia movement is the
Second Amendment to the U.S. Constitution, which
states:

> A well regulated Militia, being necessary to the security
> of a free State, the right of the people to keep and bear
> Arms, shall not be infringed.

Militia members believe that despite this constitutional guarantee, the U.S. government, of which they
are openly suspicious and resentful, is attempting to
infringe on their right to own firearms. And they see
this right as a cornerstone of other rights: if the government can disarm its citizens—which many militia
members believe it is trying to do—then it will have
free rein to do whatever it wants.

Though the beliefs of individual militia groups vary,

a common notion is that the federal government desires the integration of the United States into a "world government" administered by the United Nations. To prevent this from happening, militia members stockpile weapons and practice paramilitary maneuvers.

More than a few observers have noted that the militia movement isn't simply about protecting Second Amendment rights. Members of white supremacist hate groups have found their way into militias, and recent books have characterized the militia movement as a very real terrorist threat, perhaps the most serious terrorist threat facing the United States today.

NIGHTMARE SCENARIOS

T o anyone who might be watching, the scene is so ordinary that it would not merit a second look: two men are carrying possessions down the stairs of an apartment building and loading them into a van parked at curbside. It's life in the city—people move in, people move out.

One of the items the two men hoist into the van is an ordinary-looking steamer trunk. Actually, the trunk is lead-lined, and its contents aren't the clothes or books or dishes an observer might expect, but some wires, a timer, an explosive charge, and a metallic ball about the size of a man's fist. The ball is plutonium, a radioactive element that is the key ingredient in a nuclear bomb.

The men drive off, park the van on a side street in the city, lock the doors, and walk to a landmark where a woman is waiting for them in a car. The three then drive to the airport and within hours are on an overseas flight. Although the bomb in the steamer trunk is small

Dawning of a new age of "superterrorism"? Tokyo subway passengers await medical attention after a religious cult released sarin, a nerve gas, on crowded rush-hour trains. The 1995 terrorist attack killed 12 people and sickened about 5,500.

and crude—it contains only four kilograms, or less than nine pounds, of plutonium—it will level everything within a radius of perhaps a hundred yards, will kill thousands of people instantly, and will render a large portion of the city dangerously radioactive for more than a decade.

With countless variations, this scenario—a nuclear weapon in the hands of terrorists—inhabits the nightmares of government and law enforcement officials, as well as civilian students of terrorism. The question, of course, is how likely this scenario is to happen. Experts say that the technical knowledge necessary to build a primitive nuclear weapon isn't a real barrier. Using unclassified, publicly available information, a person with a graduate degree in physics would probably be able to design a working bomb.

The real hurdle would be obtaining a sufficient quantity of weapons-grade plutonium or uranium. One possible source would be the former Soviet Union. There, political changes have wrought economic and social chaos, leaving an unknown amount of plutonium and highly enriched uranium in insecure facilities and creating a whole class of impoverished scientists and soldiers who might be willing to steal and sell a few hundred kilograms. In his 1997 book, *The New War*, Senator John Kerry of Massachusetts, who for 10 years served as chairman or ranking member of the Senate Subcommittee on Terrorism, Narcotics, and International Operations, says that more than 800 attempts have already been made to smuggle nuclear bomb material out of the former Soviet Union. In at least 200 of these cases, the material has gotten as far as Germany. In 1995 Lithuanian officials intercepted 27 crates full of nulear bomb material destined for a buyer in Switzerland.

Concerns were heightened in September 1997, when Alexander Lebed, a former Russian general and a political opponent of President Boris Yeltsin,

announced that up to 100 suitcase-sized nuclear bombs in the Russian stockpile were unaccounted for. Though Lebed would later retract the statement, the U.S. government was concerned enough to pledge $382 million dollars within the month to help secure Russian nuclear material.

But the threat of theft is not just a concern at Russian nuclear facilities. A confidential Pentagon review that was leaked to the press in October 1997 raised "serious concerns over the status of physical security" at Department of Energy weapons-storage facilities. These concerns included insufficient guard

Japanese police surround the headquarters of Aum Shin Rikyo, the apocalyptic cult responsible for the Tokyo sarin gas attack.

forces, inadequate vaults, and malfunctioning alarms.

Despite the enormous psychological impact an atomic explosion would have, a terrorist group wouldn't necessarily need a nuclear weapon to inflict mass casualties. In fact, chemical and biological weapons are easier to make and are more portable, yet they still have the potential to kill tens of thousands of people in one attack.

A new age of "superterrorism" may well have dawned in Tokyo, Japan, on March 20, 1995. On that day, a Japanese religious cult called Aum Shin Rikyo, whose members often wrote of the impending end of the world, planted packages containing a deadly chemical agent, the nerve gas sarin, on three crowded subway lines. First developed during World War II, nerve gases interfere with the chemicals that transmit nerve impulses, causing paralysis and respiratory arrest. Fortunately for the Tokyo subway riders, sarin isn't the most lethal nerve agent; the nerve gas VX is 10 times more potent, and even the smallest exposure results in almost instantaneous death. Even so, the Tokyo sarin attack killed 12 people and sickened approximately 5,500. And the chemicals the group needed to make sarin were all legally available in Japan.

When Japanese police raided Aum Shin Rikyo's headquarters, they found documents indicating that the cult may have been contemplating a nuclear attack as well. The group apparently had been investigating the possibility of enriching the common isotope of uranium, which is useless for a bomb, into weapons-grade uranium. Although this would present a significant technical challenge, the group counted among its members a number of scientists. And buying a nuclear warhead also seemed to be an option for the well-heeled cult. Documents found at Aum's headquarters listed $200,000 as the cost for an old warhead, and $1 million as the price for a new one.

The use by terrorists of biological weapons—deadly

strains of viruses or bacteria—is also a chilling, and not too far-fetched, prospect. In the November 17, 1997, issue of *Newsweek*, Michael T. Osterholm, chief of the Minnesota Department of Health's Acute Disease Epidemiology Section, described a hypothetical biological attack at Chicago's O'Hare Airport: The terrorist leaves a briefcase in the concourse of one of the terminals. Inside the briefcase is an aerosol pump that releases botulinum, a deadly toxin, into the air. A few hours later, all the people who were in the crowded concourse start to see double and to slur their words, the first symptoms of botulism. Soon they will be completely paralyzed and will die unless placed on a ventilator. Pilots who happened to pass through the concourse are also paralyzed, and flights headed all over the world are doomed.

The possibility that terrorists would use nuclear, chemical, or biological weapons against a major population center such as Los Angeles has been the focus of much recent attention by government officials, terrorism experts, and the media.

Botulinum is an especially deadly toxin, but it is by no means the only one terrorists might use for a biological weapon. Anthrax, a dangerous bacterial agent that attacks the lungs and is relatively easy to make, would be another likely choice. Though smallpox was eradicated in 1980, the United States and the Soviet Union kept laboratory samples of the highly contagious virus, and some intelligence sources believe that disgruntled Russian scientists have stolen and sold smallpox overseas. Since no one is inoculated against it anymore, an outbreak of smallpox could be catastrophic. A researcher named Larry Wayne Harris with connections to the white supremacist group Aryan Nations even raised the specter of the "Black Death," the plague that decimated medieval Europe, when he ordered three vials of bubonic plague bacteria through the mail from a medical lab.

As with nuclear terrorism, the key question regarding chemical and biological terrorism is, what are the chances it could happen? Unfortunately, the technical hurdles aren't particularly daunting. In *The New War*, John Kerry quotes former CIA director Robert Gates on the subject: "When you talk about chemical and biological weapons in particular, a lot of them can be made in your basement, so the idea of keeping them out of terrorist hands altogether is simply not technologically feasible." But just because they could use weapons of mass destruction, does that mean terrorists necessarily *would*? A reasonable assumption is that many terrorist groups would draw the line at the massive suffering and death that a chemical or biological attack could cause. But if, for example, Ramzi Yousef was willing to kill 250,000 with a conventional bomb, is it likely that others as fanatical as he would shun mass killing with, say, a virus?

Modern terrorism has always thrived on publicity and shock value. What could generate more publicity—and strike harder at a hated enemy—than a nuclear, chemical, or biological attack? Aum Shin Rikyo may well have broken down a psychological barrier with its sarin attack on the Tokyo subway. Many analysts are asking not whether terrorists will try a similar or even more deadly operation, but where and when.

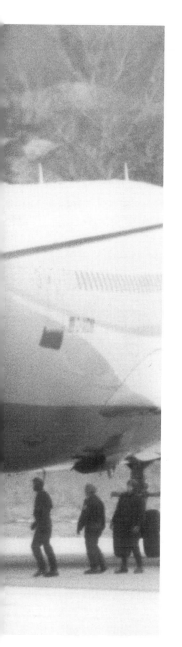

COMBATING TERRORISM IN A FREE SOCIETY

O
ne of the responsibilities of any legitimate government is to protect its people. The reality, however, is that no nation can protect all its citizens from terrorism abroad, and only a ruthless totalitarian regime can offer a reasonable guarantee of immunity from terrorism at home. In 1995, according to the U.S. State Department, 99 terrorist attacks targeted U.S. citizens or commercial or diplomatic interests abroad, resulting in the deaths of 12 American citizens; by contrast, 168 Americans died in the Oklahoma City bombing alone.

However, the Oklahoma City and World Trade Center bombings notwithstanding, the United States has witnessed comparatively little actual terrorism, and

A hostage-rescue team prepares to enter a hijacked Lufthansa jet at New York's Kennedy Airport; the hijacker surrendered and no one was injured in the incident. Responding to terrorism is a complex law enforcement, diplomatic, foreign policy, and constitutional issue.

beyond some inconvenience for international travelers, the effect of terrorism on the lives of the vast majority of ordinary citizens has been negligible. Still, there are solid reasons why even a stable and relatively terror-free society such as the United States must maintain a vigilant and vigorous stance toward terrorism.

First and, in the minds of many people, foremost is the fact that the potential use by terrorists of weapons of mass destruction—nuclear, chemical, and biological—has raised the stakes incalculably. What if, instead of detonating a truck bomb outside the Murrah building, Timothy McVeigh and Terry Nichols had decided to contaminate Oklahoma City's water supply with a deadly toxin? What if Ramzi Yousef and his companions had been able to plant a nuclear device in New York?

Second, the United States—the world's largest economy and the sole remaining superpower—has economic and political interests around the globe. This preeminence makes the United States a target for terrorists with a wide range of grievances, ranging from America's foreign policy to its perceived economic dominance to what is seen, especially in fundamentalist Islamic societies, as the decadent influence of Western cultural values. America's leadership role also makes the United States a target for governments that sponsor terrorism. The U.S. State Department estimated that, in the mid-1990s, more than 20 percent of terrorism worldwide was directed at the United States.

Failure to respond forcefully to terrorist attacks would likely encourage more terrorism. Yet in the international realm, excessive measures have the potential to alienate allies, create more (and more fanatical) enemies, and conceivably even provoke war. Confronting domestic terrorism has a different set of problems. "The basic question," Walter Laqueur has written, "is not whether [it] can be defeated; even third-rate dictatorships have shown that it can be put down with great ease. The real problem is the price to be paid by liberal

Searching for signs of trouble, an officer scans the bank of monitors covering New York's Lincoln Tunnel, one of the intended targets of the Al Salam mosque conspirators who participated in the World Trade Center bombing. Although security measures can make potential targets more difficult for terrorists to attack, protecting everyone is impossible in a free society.

societies cherishing their traditional democratic values."

After the carnage in Oklahoma City, the Clinton administration and Congress moved rapidly to counter what they characterized as a growing danger from terrorism. But many observers felt that, in their haste to appear to be doing something, politicians both overstated the real threat of terrorism and proposed remedies that would themselves threaten some of the nation's cherished liberties. In the year before the Murrah bombing, for example, the FBI reported no cases of actual or prevented terrorist incidents in the United States. In the five years before that, the FBI had recorded just 32 terrorist incidents on U.S. soil, and 9 of them—almost 30 percent—occurred on the same night, in the same city, and involved the destruction of property by animal-rights activists opposed to the selling of fur coats. The World Trade Center bombing was the only incident on U.S. soil during this period that was deemed international in origin. Meanwhile, according to the State Department, terrorist attacks outside the United States had reached a 23-year low.

Despite these figures, President Clinton and Congress proposed legislation that, critics charged, would greatly expand government powers, limit civil liberties, and weaken constitutional protections—all in the name of fighting terrorism. The proposals included an expansion of the government's authority to tap phone conversations, under some circumstances without obtaining a court order; the power to compel credit card companies, banks, hotels, and airlines to provide customer information whenever the federal government requested, also in the absence of a warrant; and the requirement that the federal government have an electronic "key" that would permit authorities to read encrypted computer messages and files as law enforcement deemed necessary. Critics felt all of these proposals were unwarranted intrusions on citizens' privacy rights.

Another provision of proposed antiterrorism legislation sought to prohibit Americans from giving any support to organizations that the secretary of state designated terrorist—even if that support was for lawful or even humanitarian purposes. If, for example, an American citizen donated clothing or books to Lebanese orphans and those donations were distributed by the political wing of Hezbollah, the American would be subject to 10 years' imprisonment. If an American paid two dollars to attend a speech by a member of the radical Jewish organization Kahane Chai, the same punishment could be applied. Civil libertarians decried the proposal as an infringement on the First Amendment rights of freedom of speech and assembly. Law professor David Cole, in an article for

The Nation titled "Terrorizing the Constitution," raised the specter of the Communist witch hunts of the 1950s, during which anyone connected with Communists or the Communist Party, even if they never supported illegal activities, was subject to harassment and prosecution. The current proposals, Cole argued, would "reintroduc[e] to criminal law the concept of guilt by association" and "authorize widespread F.B.I. political spying on nonviolent domestic organizations, an authority that history shows is bound to be abused."

Limitations on habeas corpus—by which criminal defendants have the right to appeal, in federal court, the constitutionality of their imprisonment—also found their way into antiterrorist legislation. Habeas corpus is perhaps the most important safeguard against constitutional violations in state proceedings, but under the terms of the various proposals, federal courts would have to accept the decisions of the state courts unless those decisions were clearly "arbitrary" and "unreasonable." Because the habeas corpus limitations applied to all state crimes, and because a defendant appealing for a writ of habeas corpus is by definition already in custody, critics wondered how the changes would prevent terrorism.

Critics also wondered about the wisdom of provisions for deporting immigrants suspected of belonging to terrorist groups. Proposed legislation would set up a special five-judge court appointed by the Chief Justice of the United States to hear all such alien-removal cases. In these hearings, the Federal Rules of Evidence would not apply: secret evidence could be submitted by the Justice Department, with the suspected terrorist being informed only of the general charges against him or her (this, proponents claimed, was necessary to protect the source of the information), and unlawfully obtained evidence would be admissible. Some legal scholars likened such an arrangement to the Star Chamber, a feared court that the British monarchy had used to stifle opposition and whose use of secret evidence had made it virtually impossible for the accused to mount a defense.

Because of heated opposition from civil libertarians and legal scholars, many of the controversial proposals were eliminated from the final version of the Antiterrorism and Effective Death Penalty Act of 1996, which Congress passed in the wake of the Oklahoma City bombing. For example, instead of expanding the FBI's wiretapping powers, the bill ordered the attorney general to study the issue; and the government was not given the authority to have an electronic key for reading encrypted computer messages. But habeas corpus restrictions were enacted, as was a prohibition on giving "material support or resources," except medicine or religious materials, to foreign organizations designated terrorist; and the special alien-removal court, complete with provisions for the use of secret evidence, was set up to deal with immigrants suspected of having ties to terrorist groups.

That protection against terrorism carries a cost in reduced rights and freedoms is fairly obvious. The question is, what level of protection do we want and how much are we willing to pay for it? Prohibiting support for even the lawful activities of groups the U.S. government designates terrorist or permitting secret evidence to be used in alien-removal hearings might not seem like too high a price to pay for reducing the terrorist threat, but critics worry about the balance of government power and individual liberties, and they fear an erosion of our long-held, cherished freedoms. If the government can punish citizens for merely associating with foreign groups it has designated terrorist, what's to prevent the government at some later point from prohibiting association with dissident groups at home? If secret evidence is admissible in deportation hearings because the identity of an informant must be protected, why can't secret information be used in, say, a drug trial when sources in an ongoing drug investigation must also be protected? The danger, civil libertarians argue, is that the individual protections the government takes away for the limited purpose of fighting terrorism will gradually be taken away in other areas as well. If that notion seems far-fetched, just look at Great Britain, civil libertarians say.

In October 1974 IRA bombs exploded in two pubs in Birmingham, killing 21 people. The British Parliament reacted by unanimously passing the Prevention of Terrorism Bill, which was supposed to expire after a year but which Parliament renewed year after year. The bill permitted police to stop and search, without a warrant, anyone suspected of terrorism. It allowed suspects to be detained for 48 hours without charge, and that period could be extended by five days upon authorization by the secretary of state. The secretary of state also could issue an order prohibiting a citizen from entering a specified part of the British Isles, such as Ireland, and the person had no right to hear the evidence upon which that decision had been based. Organizing or attending a meeting at which a member of the IRA spoke was illegal, as was the mere wearing of clothes showing support for the IRA.

Over the years additional government powers and restrictions on individual liberties were added. "One of the most important lessons from Britain," David Kopel, a policy analyst from the Cato Institute, told the U.S. Senate Judiciary Committee, "is that even a huge dose of restrictions on civil liberties, such as the Prevention of Terrorism Bill, does not long remain 'sufficient' in the eyes of the government. At least in regard to civil liberties, the Domino Theory has proven correct, as one traditional Anglo-American freedom after another has fallen under the government's assertion of the need for still more anti-terrorist powers."

Among the more troubling changes were the following: In Northern Ireland the right to a jury trial

In its desire to stamp out Irish terrorism, the British Parliament adopted a host of restrictions on civil liberties, the rights of suspects, and freedom of the press. One of the more absurd was the prohibition against broadcasting the voice or image of Gerry Adams (right), the president of Sinn Fein.

was suspended for those accused of political violence. Confessions were deemed admissible without corroboration even though they were routinely obtained through the use of such techniques as sleep and food deprivation, placing a hood over the suspect's head, and making the suspect stand against a wall for long periods. For the first time, a suspect's decision to remain silent could be used as evidence against him or her in court—and not just in cases of suspected terrorism, either. If authorized by the secretary of state, police could break into any house, steal or destroy private property, commit arson, even leave planted evidence—all with impunity. And the press was muzzled as well: TV stations were forbidden from broadcasting not only statements by IRA terrorists, but also statements by representatives of Sinn Fein, a legal political party. Stations were forced to hire actors to read the words of Sinn Fein's president, Gerry Adams, because it was illegal to broadcast his image or voice; for a while it was also against the law to show archival footage of Eamon De Valera, Ireland's first president.

The sad irony is that none of these changes seemed to have much effect on terrorism in Northern Ireland. And yet Great Britain is a lot less free today than it was 20 or 25 years ago, which, American civil libertarians say, should strike a note of caution among those who would diminish the Bill of Rights in the name of combating terrorism.

But dealing with the terrorist threat is not simply a question of finding the proper balance of security and freedom at home. It is also a complex intelligence-gathering, law enforcement, and foreign policy challenge. In the United States, the FBI is charged with the prevention and investigation of domestic terrorism, and at least part of the credit for the low incidence of terrorism on American soil must go to the bureau's effectiveness in carrying out this mission. The record of America's intelligence community in uncovering international terrorist threats is more mixed. The task requires both the gathering of relevant information and the correct interpretation of that information. Getting information about terrorists' plans often requires having human sources—informers and spies—in the midst of the terrorists. But this presents many difficulties, as Stansfield Turner, former director of the CIA, has noted:

> Spies cannot be recruited overnight. A suitable candidate must be identified, his friendship and trust nurtured over weeks and months until he is willing to work for us, an opportunity found to insert him in the organizations we

want to learn about, and enough time allowed him to gain the trust of that organization. . . . And terrorist groups are usually composed of fanatics who are not easily fooled by imposters.

One of the most abject failures of U.S. intelligence occurred in the late 1970s, when the success of the Shiite Muslim revolution in Iran caught the CIA completely off guard. The CIA, which lacked well-placed Iranian sources who might have provided timely intelligence, also misinterpreted the information it did have, concluding that the U.S.-supported shah of Iran would easily weather the unrest in his country because he controlled the nation's military and secret police. But in February 1979, while the shah was overseas, the last vestiges of his regime collapsed, and Shiite revolutionaries led by the Ayatollah Ruhollah Khomeini took power. The new Iranian government proved extremely anti-Western and anti-American. Militants seized the American embassy in Tehran in November, taking embassy staff hostage and demanding that the United States return the shah to his homeland to stand trial. The United States refused, and what followed was a protracted hostage crisis that revealed America's impotence in dealing with this kind of terrorism and cost President Jimmy Carter any chance for reelection.

When intelligence and law enforcement agencies fail to head off a terrorist threat and an actual attack occurs, the first priority is finding out who was responsible, gathering enough evidence for an arrest, and proving the case to a jury in court. Because a terrorist act may involve various individuals and may be carried out with no claim of responsibility or with responsibility claimed by a nonexistent organization, this can be a difficult task even when the terrorists are homegrown and can theoretically be more easily monitored.

When those responsible are international terrorists, the obstacles are even greater. Before investigators can establish what caused an explosion, for example, the

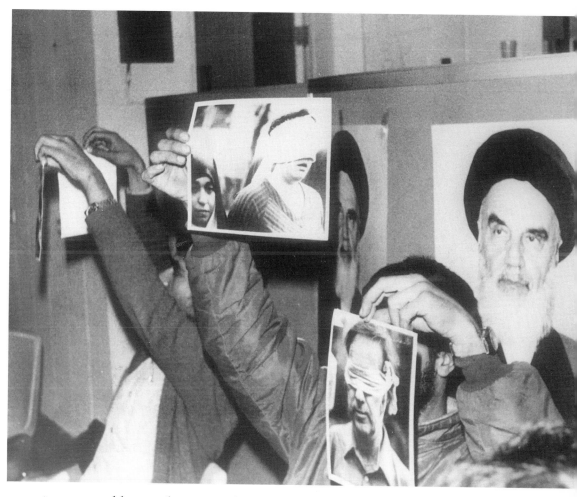

terrorist responsible may be in another country, living under another name. And even if they knew that he was a terrorist, the people there might be sympathetic to his viewpoint or have some family or clan ties to him. To loosen such personal sympathies and loyalties, the U.S. State Department established a fund to reward people for information leading to the apprehension of terrorists. And the strategy has paid big dividends. The $2 million reward for information about Ramzi Yousef, for example, was a decisive factor in his capture in Pakistan.

But finding out who the terrorist is and where he's

Backed by posters of the Ayatollah Khomeini, Islamic militants display photos of blindfolded American hostages shortly after the takeover of the U.S. embassy in Tehran, Iran, in 1979. The hostage crisis reflected an abject failure by U.S. intelligence.

living doesn't always guarantee that he'll be brought to justice. For one thing, the nation where he lives might not extradite criminals. The Clinton administration has made increased use of extradition a component of its antiterrorism strategy; it has sought to negotiate new and more comprehensive extradition treaties with more than 20 nations.

Extradition is but a small piece in the mosaic of world terrorism, however. Of vastly greater significance (and much more problematic to democratic governments) is the phenomenon of state-sponsored terrorism. Various nations give support to terrorist organizations, ranging from financial aid to safe haven to the provision of training bases, weapons, or technical assistance from national intelligence services. In some cases, terrorists are little more than contract agents, carrying out operations ordered and directed by their sponsoring government. The Abu Nidal group, for example, has done the bidding of several Arab governments—in return for hefty fees. Libya's Muammar Gadhafi, the leader by far the most open in his support for terrorism, actually advertised, in Arabic-language newspapers, for terrorists willing to do his bidding. Lebanese sources during the 1980s revealed that Gadhafi even had a more or less fixed pay scale, depending on the mission. For example, a suicide bomber would earn 300,000 Lebanese pounds (to be paid to his family).

All of this complicates the task of fighting terrorism enormously. In some cases the identity of the group that carried out an operation can be established, but who actually ordered it remains unclear. In other cases individual suspects are identified but can't be brought to justice because they are protected by a state sponsor (this is the situation with the men believed responsible for the Pan Am Flight 103 bombing, who were still being sheltered by Libya as of spring 1998). In still other cases there is good evidence of a government's involvement in planning or carrying out a terrorist attack but no way to bring the decision makers responsible to justice.

The U.S. government's response to state-sponsored terrorism has been primarily diplomatic and economic. The State Department issues a list each year of governments involved in supporting terrorism, and those nations are subject to diplomatic and economic sanctions. Unfortunately, these kinds of sanctions are effective only when observed over an extended period by the entire world community, a rare occurrence.

Desiring more immediate and forceful ways to counter terrorism, many nations created special military units. In the 1970s, a slew of airplane hijacking and hostage situations made hostage rescue a primary function of these units, but they were supposed to be able to respond quickly to various terrorist contingencies.

In many ways the model for antiterrorist units came from Israel, whose General Intelligence and Reconnaissance Unit Number 269 was responsible for releasing 90 hostages aboard a hijacked Sabena airliner at Israel's Lod Airport in 1972. But the Israelis pulled off an even more spectacular feat four years later, when pro-Palestinian terrorists hijacked an Air France flight from Tel Aviv to Paris and diverted the plane to Entebbe Airport in the central African nation of Uganda. The terrorists demanded the release of 53 Palestinian prisoners being held in Israel and Europe and warned that they would begin executing the more than 100 mostly Israeli hostages if their demands weren't met. Not only was Uganda more than 2,000 miles away, but its government was sympathetic to the Palestinian cause, and Ugandan soldiers actually helped the terrorists guard their hostages.

On the night of July 3, 1976, Israeli forces flew to Uganda aboard three C-130 Hercules military transport planes, which landed without lights on a plain near Entebbe Airport. The Israeli commandos quickly proceeded to the airport terminal, where they surprised the terrorists and their Ugandan allies. In the ensuing battle, seven terrorists, about 20 Ugandan soldiers, three hostages, and one Israeli commando were killed. Within an hour of the initial landing, the Israeli fighters and 103 freed hostages were in the air again, headed for safety.

In March 1978, President Jimmy Carter created the Delta Force, an elite U.S. military unit with antiterrorist responsibilities. On April 24, 1980, the Delta Force, which draws volunteers from all branches of the military, launched a hostage-rescue mission thousands of miles from American soil, but unlike the Israeli raid on Entebbe, this operation would fail. Operation Eagle Claw was supposed to free the 53 American hostages held in Tehran, but the mission had to be aborted in the northern deserts of Iran after a helicopter and a cargo plane collided, killing eight members of the rescue team. The failed raid proved a propaganda bonanza for Iran and a humiliating blow to America's image.

The United States had more success in 1985. On October 7 of that year, four PLO terrorists hijacked an Italian passenger ship, the *Achille Lauro*, and ordered it to Egypt. Along the way, they murdered an American tourist, Leon Klinghoffer, and dumped his body into the Mediterranean Sea. In Egypt, the terrorists traded their hostages for a Egypt Air jet to take them to Tunisia. Using sophisticated U.S.-provided signals intelligence (SIGINT) technology, which combines lasers, satellites, and electronic monitoring of radio transmissions, Israeli intelligence furnished the United States with the departure time and tail markings of the hijackers' jet. U.S. AWACS electronic surveillance planes then located the jet, even though it was night-time, and directed navy F-14 fighter planes on a course to intercept it. The F-14s forced the commercial jet to land at a NATO base in Italy, where Italian authorities arrested the hijackers.

In addition to using military force to resolve terrorist crises as they unfold, nations have the option of launching retaliatory strikes in the wake of a terrorist attack. Israel, perhaps because of its unique position as a land surrounded by enemies and besieged by terrorists, has been the only country to routinely respond to terrorism with overt military force. Israeli retaliation for terrorism has often included the shelling and bombing of Palestinian refugee camps—the terrorists' base of support but also the home of innocent noncombatants, including women and children. Israel even invaded the neighboring country of Lebanon in June 1982 in an effort to expel the PLO from its headquarters in Beirut. It seems doubtful that such actions deterred future terrorists. Indeed, many observers believe that Israel's

The Achille Lauro docks in Egypt after Palestinian terrorists had hijacked the Italian cruise ship en route to Israel and murdered an American passenger. The combined efforts of the United States, Israel, and Italy led to the terrorists' apprehension.

harsh responses have only bred more anti-Israeli fanaticism.

The U.S. history of military retaliation for terrorism is limited. On April 5, 1986, a bomb exploded at La Belle, a discotheque in West Berlin that was popular with off-duty American servicemen. Two people, including one American serviceman, were killed in the blast, and about 60 Americans were among the more than 200 wounded. Intercepted messages between Libya's intelligence agency and its embassy in East Berlin seemed to conclusively establish Libyan involvement. The Reagan administration, long irked by Libyan leader Muammar Gadhafi's open support of terrorism, decided to act.

Just before 2:00 A.M. on April 15, about 30 United States Air Force and Navy warplanes entered Libyan airspace traveling at 540 miles per hour only 200 feet above the ground. The bombers' targets were the port city of Benghazi and the capital, Tripoli, with special attention to be paid to Gadhafi's compound on the Sidi Balal naval base. As one group of planes attacked the military airfield in Tripoli, another dropped 2,000-pound, laser-guided bombs on the dictator's barracks. The Libyans claimed 37 dead, including Gadhafi's adopted daughter, and 93 wounded, including two of his sons. Gadhafi himself had been sleeping outside in a tent and was unhurt.

The raid wasn't well received by the international community. The Arab nations condemned it. Even Western allies failed to support America's actions; with the exception of Great Britain, every country had, in fact, denied the U.S. planes permission to enter their airspace. At home, however, the attack was quite popular. Although it hadn't accomplished what had clearly been a major goal—killing Gadhafi—the raid had, Americans widely believed, sent a message to the Libyan dictator as well as to other nations who sponsored terrorism.

"Today we have done what we had to do," President Ronald Reagan said in a TV address only hours after the raid had been completed. "If necessary, we shall do it again."

But neither Reagan nor his successors, George Bush and Bill Clinton, did do it again, even when strong evidence pointed to the involvement of other nations, such as Syria and Iran, in terrorist attacks against U.S. targets. The military response to state-sponsored terrorism simply has too many drawbacks for the United States. Libya is a militarily weak and diplomatically marginal country; an attack on, for example, Syria

Firemen inspect La Belle, a West Berlin discotheque frequented by American servicemen, after a bomb had exploded inside, killing 2 people and wounding more than 200. Intercepted messages pointed to the involvement of Libya in the attack.

would be much riskier and might spark retaliation against Israel. Plus, the United States cannot afford to alienate allies, especially in the Arab world, because it needs their help to achieve important foreign policy goals, such as Arab-Israeli peace and the containment of Iraq.

If military retaliation against terrorists and their sponsors is generally impractical, covert, or secret, action seems to hold wider promise. In 1984 the CIA was given a new directive—to adopt a more proactive role in the fight against terrorism. The CIA was to carry out covert operations to destabilize or even topple governments that supported terrorism. It was also to sow discord among various terrorist groups so that they would spend their time fighting each other rather than attacking Americans. A decade later, the Antiterrorism and Effective Death Penalty Act of 1996 reinforced this mandate, saying that "the President should use all necessary means, including covert action and military force, to disrupt, dismantle, and destroy international infrastructure used by international terrorists, including overseas terrorist training facilities and safe havens. . . ."

Many Americans feel ambivalent about their government engaging in covert operations. On the one hand, if a ruthless foe has shown itself willing to shed innocent blood through covert means, and the only practical way to fight that enemy is through covert means, then the undertaking seems justified. On the other hand, experience has shown that the rationale for covert operations, and the tactics used, tend to be a bit less clear morally. When, during the 1970s, the excesses of past CIA operations came to light in congressional hearings, many Americans were outraged.

But precisely where should the line be drawn with secret operations against terrorists? With destruction of infrastructure such as training bases? With kidnapping? With murder?

Israel's response has always been clear and un-

equivocal. The Mossad, the Israeli counterpart to the American CIA, fights terror with terror. After the 1972 Munich Olympics attack, Mossad assassination squads fanned out across Europe and killed Black September leaders. In the 1970s and 1980s PLO officials were assassinated in various countries (and on occasion their families were also killed). Letter bombs were sent to terrorist leaders. Shiite terrorist leaders were kidnapped from foreign countries and held in Israel. More recently, a Palestinian bomb maker named Yehiya Ayyash was killed in January 1996 by a booby-trapped cellular phone. On September 25, 1997, Mossad agents traveled to Amman, Jordan, to assassinate Khalid

America's CIA director, in conjunction with a Saudi Arabian ambassador, sponsored a 1985 assassination attempt against Sheik Mohammed Hussein Fadlallah (above), the head of Hezbollah. Fadlallah escaped the assassination attempt unscathed, but 80 people were killed by the massive car bomb.

Mashaal, a leader of the militant Hamas organization. After injecting Mashaal with poison, however, the agents were caught, and Israel was forced to provide the antidote. The incident strained relations with Jordan's King Hussein, a moderate Arab leader, embarrassed the Israeli government, and precipitated the resignation of the Mossad's chief.

The Mashaal debacle illustrates the political dangers of covert operations. But beyond the potential fallout from a publicly exposed mission, many Americans would question the moral rectitude of assassinations, even when the targets have ties to terrorist groups. And indeed, an executive order (an order from the president) prohibiting political assassinations during peacetime has been in effect since 1981. But in at least one instance, according to journalist Bob Woodward, that directive was ignored in the name of counterterrorist goals.

Sheik Mohammed Hussein Fadlallah, a radical Shiite cleric, was the founder of Hezbollah, a Lebanon-based, anti-Israeli, anti-American group. Hezbollah and Fadlallah were linked to several terrorist attacks against Americans, including the bombing of the Marine barracks in Beirut. CIA director William Casey decided that Fadlallah had to be eliminated, Woodward revealed in his 1987 book *Veil*. With $3 million from the Saudi Arabian government, a former member of Britain's elite Special Air Services was hired to kill the sheik. On March 8, 1985, the assassination attempt was made using a huge car bomb parked about 50 yards from Fadlallah's Beirut apartment building. The blast collapsed buildings, killed 80 people, and wounded some 200 others, but Fadlallah emerged unhurt.

Even if the assassination attempt had succeeded, the indiscriminate carnage would have raised troubling moral questions. The operation was itself an act of terrorism, indistinguishable from the anti-American attacks its target had encouraged or sponsored. The mangled limbs and lifeless eyes of innocent civilians who perished in the bombing were a stark reminder that, in the battle against terrorism, there is a real danger of losing sight of the very values a free nation is supposedly fighting to preserve.

Further Reading

Charters, David A., ed. *The Deadly Sin of Terrorism*. Westport, Conn.: Greenwood Press, 1994.

Gearty, Conor. *Terror*. London: Faber and Faber, 1991.

Jeffreys, Diarmuid. *The Bureau: Inside the Modern FBI*. Boston: Houghton Mifflin, 1995.

Laqueur, Walter. *The Age of Terrorism*. Boston: Little, Brown and Co., 1987.

Mullins, Wayman C. *Terrorist Organizations in the United States*. Springfield, Ill.: Charles C. Thomas Publishers, 1988.

Schlagheck, Donna M. *International Terrorism*. Lexington, Mass.: Lexington Books, 1988.

Seale, Patrick. *Abu Nidal: A Gun for Hire*. New York: Random House, 1992.

Taylor, Peter. *States of Terror: Democracy and Political Violence*. London: BBC Books, 1991.

Wolf, John B. *Antiterrorist Initiatives*. New York: Plenum Press, 1989.

Index

ANN G. GAINES, a freelance writer who lives in Gonzales, Texas, is the author of a half-dozen books for young adults. She has master's degrees in Library Science and American Civilization from the University of Texas at Austin.

AUSTIN SARAT is William Nelson Cromwell Professor of Jurisprudence and Political Science at Amherst College, where he also chairs the Department of Law, Jurisprudence and Social Thought. Professor Sarat is the author or editor of 23 books and numerous scholarly articles. Among his books are *Law's Violence, Sitting in Judgment: Sentencing the White Collar Criminal*, and *Justice and Injustice in Law and Legal Theory*. He has received many academic awards and held several prestigious fellowships. He is President of the Law & Society Association and Chair of the Working Group on Law, Culture and the Humanities. In addition, he is a nationally recognized teacher and educator whose teaching has been featured in the *New York Times*, on the *Today* show, and on National Public Radio's *Fresh Air*.

Picture Credits